TOM SLADE
AT BLACK LAKE

PERCY KEESE FITZHUGH

1st WORLD
LIBRARY
Literary Society

Tom Slade at Black Lake

Percy Keese Fitzhugh

© 1st World Library, 2006
PO Box 2211
Fairfield, IA 52556
www.1stworldlibrary.com
First Edition

LCCN: 2006907728

Softcover ISBN: 1-4218-2448-5
Hardcover ISBN: 1-4218-2348-9
eBook ISBN: 1-4218-2548-1

Purchase *"Tom Slade at Black Lake"*
as a traditional bound book at:
www.1stWorldLibrary.com/purchase.asp?ISBN=1-4218-2448-5

1st World Library is a literary, educational organization
dedicated to:

- Creating a free internet library of downloadable ebooks

  - Hosting writing competitions and offering book
    publishing scholarships.

Interested in more 1st World Library books?
contact: literacy@1stworldlibrary.com
Check us out at: www.1stworldlibrary.com

1st World Library Literary Society

Giving Back to the World

"If you want to work on the core problem, it's early school literacy."

- James Barksdale, former CEO of Netscape

"No skill is more crucial to the future of a child, or to a democratic and prosperous society, than literacy."

- Los Angeles Times

Literacy... means far more than learning how to read and write... The aim is to transmit... knowledge and promote social participation."

- UNESCO

"Literacy is not a luxury, it is a right and a responsibility. If our world is to meet the challenges of the twenty-first century we must harness the energy and creativity of all our citizens."

- President Bill Clinton

"Parents should be encouraged to read to their children, and teachers should be equipped with all available techniques for teaching literacy, so the varying needs and capacities of individual kids can be taken into account."

- Hugh Mackay

PREFACE

Several persons have asked me when Tom Slade was ever going to grow up and cease to be a Scout. The answer is that he is already grown up and that he is never going to cease to be a Scout. Once a Scout, always a Scout. To hear some people talk one would think that scouting is like the measles; that you get over it and never have it any more.

Scouting is not a thing to play with, like a tin steam-engine, and then to throw aside. If you once get caught in the net of scouting, you will never disentangle yourself. A fellow may grow up and put on long trousers and go and call on a girl and all that sort of thing, but if he was a Scout, he will continue to be a Scout, and it will stick out all over him. You'll find him back in the troop as assistant or scoutmaster or something or other.

I think Tom Slade is a very good example. He left the troop to go and work on a transport; he got into the motorcycle messenger service; he became one of the greatest daredevils of the air; he came home quite "grown up" as you would say, and knuckled down to be a big business man.

Then, when it came to a show down, what did he do? He found out that he was just a plain Scout, shouldered his axe, and went off and did a big scout job all alone. So there you are.

I am sorry for those who would have him too old for scouting, and who seem to think that a fellow can lay aside all he has learned in the woods and in the handbook, the same as he can lay aside his short trousers. It isn't as easy as all that.

Did you suppose that Tom Slade was going to get acquainted with nature, with the woods and streams and trees, and make them his friends, and then repudiate these friends?

Do you think that a Scout is a quitter?

Tom Slade was always a queer sort of duck, and goodness only knows what he will do next. He may go to the North Pole for all I know. But one thing you may be sure of; he is still a Scout of the Scouts, and if you think he is too old to be a Scout, then how about Buffalo Bill?

The fact is that Tom is just beginning to reap the real harvest of scouting. The best is yet to come, as Pee-wee Harris usually observes, just before dessert is served at dinner. If it is any satisfaction to you to know it, Tom is more of a Scout than at any time in his career, and there is a better chance of his being struck by lightening than his drifting away from the troop whose adventures you have followed with his.

It is true that Tom has grown faster than his companions and found it necessary to go to work while they are still at school. And this very circumstance will enable us to see what scouting has done for him.

Indeed if I could not show you that, then all of those eight stores of his adventures would have been told to little purpose. The chief matter of interest about a trail is where it leads to. It may be an easy trail or a hard trail, but the question is, where does it go to?

It would be a fine piece of business, I think, to leave Tom sitting on a rock near the end of the trail without giving you so much as a glimpse of what is at the end of it.

So you may tell your parents and your teachers and your uncles and your aunts not to worry about Tom Slade never growing up. He is just a trifle over eighteen years old and very strong and husky. Confidentially, I look upon him as nothing but a kid. I keep tabs on his age and when he has to go on crutches and is of no more interest to you, I shall be the first to know it. He is likely to have no end of adventures between eighteen and twenty.

Meanwhile, don't worry about him. He's just a big overgrown kid and the best Scout this side of Mars.

P. K. F.

CONTENTS

CHAPTER I

TOM LOOKS AT THE MAP

Tom Slade, bending over the office table, scrutinized the big map of Temple Camp. It was the first time he had really looked at it since his return from France, and it made him homesick to see, even in its cold outlines, the familiar things and scenes which he had so loved as a scout. The hill trail was nothing but a dotted line, but Tom knew it for more than that, for it was along its winding way into the dark recesses of the mountains that he had qualified for the pathfinder's badge. Black Lake was just an irregular circle, but in his mind's eye he saw there the moonlight glinting up the water, and canoes gliding silently, and heard the merry voices of scouts diving from the springboard at its edge.

He liked this map better than maps of billets and trenches, and to him the hill trail was more suggestive of adventure than the Hindenburg Line. He had been very close to the Hindenburg Line and it had meant no more to him than the equator. He had found the war to be like a three-ringed circus - it was too big. Temple Camp was about the right size.

Tom reached for a slip of paper and laying it upon the map just where the trail went over the hilltop and off the camp territory altogether, jotted down the numbers of three cabins which were indicated by little squares.

"They're the only three together and kind of separate," he said to himself.

Then he went over to the window and gazed out upon the busy scene, which the city office of Temple Camp overlooked. He did this, not because there was anything there which he wished particularly to see, but because he contemplated doing something and was in some perplexity about it. He was going to dictate a letter to Miss Margaret Ellison, the stenographer.

Tom had seen cannons and machine guns and hand grenades and depth bombs, but the thing in all this world that he was most afraid of was the long sharply pointed pencil which Miss Margaret Ellison always held poised above her open note book, waiting to record his words. Tom had always fallen down at the last minute and told her what he wanted to say; suggesting that she say it in her own sweet way. He did not say *sweet* way, though he may have thought it.

So now he stood at the open window looking down upon Bridgeboro's surging thoroughfare, while the breath of Spring permeated the Temple Camp office. If he had been less susceptible of this gentle influence in the very air, he would still have known it was Spring by the things in the store windows across the way - straw hats and hammocks and tennis rackets. There were moving vans, too, with furniture bulging out behind them, which are just as certain signs of merry May as the flowers that bloom in the Spring. There was something too, in the way that the sun moved down which bespoke Spring.

But the surest sign of all was the flood of applications for cabin accommodations at Temple Camp; that was just as sure and reliable as the first croaking of the frogs or the softening of the rich, thick mud in Barrel Alley, where Tom had spent his childhood.

He moved over to where Miss Margaret Ellison sat at her machine. Mr. Burton, manager of the Temple Camp office, had told Tom that the only way to acquire confidence and readiness of speech was to formulate what he wished to say and to say it, without depending on any one else, and to this good advice, Peewee Harris, mascot of Tom's Scout Troop had made the additional suggestion, that it was good to say it whether you had anything to say or not, on the theory, I suppose, that if you cannot shoot bullets, it is better to shoot blank cartridges than nothing at all.

CHAPTER II

HE SENDS A LETTER

"Help him, but encourage him to be self-confident; let him take responsibilities. He understands everything well enough; all he needs is to get a grip on himself." That is what Mr. Burton had told Margaret Ellison, and Margaret Ellison, being a girl, understood better than all the army surgeons in the country.

You see how it was; they had made a wreck of Tom Slade's nerves as a trifling incidental to making the world safe for democracy. He started at every little noise, he broke down in the middle of his talk, he hesitated to cross the street alone, he shuddered at the report of a bursting tire on some unlucky auto. He had never been at ease in the presence of girls, and he was now less at ease than before he had gone away.

He had fought for nearly two years and Uncle Sam liked him so much that he could not bring himself to part company with him, until by hook or crook, Mr. Burton and Mr. Temple managed to get him discharged and put him in the way of finding himself at his old job in Temple Camp office. It was a great relief to him not to have to salute lieutenants any more. The shot and shell he did not mind, but his arm was weary with saluting lieutenants. It was the dream of Tom Slade's life never to see another lieutenant as long as he lived.

He leaned against the table near Miss Margaret Ellison and

said, "I - I want - I have to send a letter to a troop that's in Ohio - in a place called - called Dansburg. Shall I dic - shall I say what I want to tell them?"

"Surely," she said cheerily.

"Maybe if it isn't just right you can fix it up," he said.

"You say it just the way you want to," she encouraged him.

"It's to the Second Dansburg Troop and the name of the scoutmaster is William Barnard," Tom said, "and this is what I want to say...."

"Yes, say it in your own words," she reminded him.

"We got - I mean received," he dictated hesitatingly, "your letter and we can give you - can give you - three cabins - three cabins together and kind of separate like you say - numbers five, six, and seven. They are on the hill and separate, and we hope to hear from you - soon - because there are lots of troops asking for cabins, because now the season is beginning. Yours truly."

"Is that all right?" he asked rather doubtfully.

"Surely it is," she said; "and don't forget what Mr. Burton told you about going home early and resting. Remember, Mr. Burton is your superior officer now."

"Are you going home soon?" he asked her.

"Not till half-past five," she said.

He hesitated as if he would like to say something more, then retreating rather clumsily, he got his hat and said good-night, and left the office.

The letter which he had dictated was not laid upon Mr.

Burton's desk for signature in exactly the phraseology which Tom had used, but Tom never knew that. This is the way the letter read:

MR. WILLIAM BARNARD, Scoutmaster,
Second Dansburg Troop,
Dansburg, Ohio.

DEAR SIR,

Replying to your letter asking for accommodations for your three patrols for month of August, we can assign you three cabins (Numbers, 5,6 and 7) covering that time. These are in an isolated spot, as you requested, being somewhat removed from the body of the camp.

Circular of rates and particulars is enclosed. Kindly answer promptly, as applications are numerous.

Yours truly,

The letter went out that night, and as it happened, a very considerable series of adventures resulted.

Perhaps if Margaret Ellison had looked at the map or even stopped to think, she would have consulted with Tom before typing that letter, which was the cause of such momentous consequences. As for Mr. Burton, he knew that Tom knew the camp like A. B. C. and he simply signed his name to the letter and let it go at that.

CHAPTER III

THE NEW STRUGGLE

Tom did as he had promised Mr. Burton he would do; he went home and lay down and rested. It was not much of a home, but it was better than a dugout. That is, it was cleaner though not very much larger. But there were no lieutenants.

It was a tiny hall-room in a boarding house, and the single window afforded a beautiful view of back fences. It was all the home that Tom Slade knew. He had no family, no relations, nothing.

He had been born in a tenement in Barrel Alley, where his mother had died and from which his good-for-nothing father had disappeared. For a while he had been a waif and a hoodlum, and by strict attention to the code of Barrel Alley's gang, he had risen to be king of the hoodlums. No one, not even Blokey Mattenburg himself, could throw a rock into a trolley car with the precision of Tom Slade.

Then, on an evil day, he was tempted to watch the scouts and it proved fatal. He was drawn head over ears into scouting, and became leader of the new Elk Patrol in the First Bridgeboro Troop. For three seasons he was a familiar, if rather odd figure, at Temple Camp, which Mr. John Temple of Bridgeboro had founded in the Catskills, and when he was old enough to work it seemed natural that these kindly gentlemen who had his welfare at heart, should put him into the city office of the camp, which he left to go to war, and to which he had but lately returned, suffering from shell-shock.

He was now eighteen years old, and though no longer a scout in the ordinary sense, he retained his connection with the troop in capacity of assistant to Mr. Ellsworth, the troop's scoutmaster.

He had been rather older than the members of this troop when he made his spectacular leap from hoodlumism to scouting, and hence while they were still kicking their heels in the arena he had, as one might say, passed outside it.

But his love for the boys and their splendid scoutmaster who had given him a lift, was founded upon a rock. The camp and the troop room had been his home, the scouts had been his brothers, and all the simple associations of his new life were bound up with these three patrols.

Perhaps it was for this reason that among these boys, all younger than himself, and with whom he had always mingled on such familiar terms, he showed but few, and those not often, of the distressing symptoms which bespoke his shattered nerves. Among them he found refuge and was at peace with himself.

And the boys, intent upon their own pursuits, knew nothing of the brave struggle he was making at the office where his days were spent, and in the poor little shabbily furnished room where he would lie down on his iron bed and try to rest and forget the war and not hear the noises outside.

How he longed for Friday nights when the troop met, and when he could forget himself in those diverting games!

Since the first few days of his return from France, he had seen but little of the troop, except upon those gala nights. The boys were in school and he at the office, and it seemed as if their two ways had parted, after all his hopes that his return might find them reunited and more intimate than ever before. But after the first joyous welcome, it had not been so. It could not be so.

Of course, if they had known how he loved to just sit and listen to them jolly the life out of Peewee Harris, they would doubtless have arranged to do this every night for his amusement, for it made no difference to them how much they jollied Peewee. If they had had the slightest inkling that it helped him just to listen to Roy Blakeley's nonsense, they would probably have arranged with Roy for a continuous performance, for so far as Roy was concerned, there was no danger of a shortage of nonsense. But you see they did not think of these things.

They did much for wounded soldiers, but Tom Slade was not a wounded soldier. And so it befell that the very thing which he most needed was the thing he did not have, and that was just the riot of banter and absurdity which they called their meetings. At all this he would just sit and smile and forget to interlace his fingers and jerk his head. And sometimes he would even laugh outright.

I am afraid that everything was managed wrong from the first. It would have been better if Mr. Burton or Mr. Ellsworth or somebody or other had told the troop the full truth about Tom's condition. I suppose they refrained for fear the boys would stare at him and treat him as one stricken, and thereby, perhaps make his struggle harder.

At all events, it was hard enough. And little they knew of this new and frightful war that he was struggling through with all the power of his brave, dogged nature. Little they knew how he lay awake night after night, starting at every chime of the city's clock, of how he did the best he could each day, waiting and longing for Friday night, hoping, *hoping* that Peewee and Roy would surely be there. Poor, distracted, shell-shocked fighter that he was, he was fighting still, and they were his only hope and they did not know it. No one knew it. He would not let them know.

For that was Tom Slade.

CHAPTER IV

"LUCKY LUKE"

Next morning Tom had his breakfast in a dingy little restaurant and then started along Terrace Avenue for the bank building, in which was the Temple Camp office.

He still wore the shabby khaki uniform which had seen service at the front. He was of that physique called thick-set and his face was of the square type, denoting doggedness and endurance, and a stolid temperament.

There had never been anything suggestive of the natty or agile about him when he had been a scout, and army life, contrary to its reputation, had not spruced and straightened him up at all. He was about as awkward looking as a piece of field artillery, and he was just about as reliable and effective. He was not built on the lines of a rifle, but rather on the lines of a cannon, or perhaps of a tank. His mouth was long and his lips set tight, but it twitched nervously at one end, especially when he waited at the street crossing just before he reached the bank building, watching the traffic with a kind of fearful, bewildered look.

Twice, thrice, he made the effort to cross and returned to his place on the curb, interlacing his fingers distractedly. And yet this young fellow had pushed through barbed wire entanglements and gone across No Man's Land, without so much as a shudder in the very face of hostile fire.

He always dreaded this street corner in the mornings and was thankful when he was safe up in his beloved Temple Camp office. If he had been on crutches some grateful citizen would have helped him across, and patriotic young ladies would have paused to watch the returned hero and some one might even have removed his hat in the soldier's presence; for they did those things - for a while.

But such honors were only for those who were fortunate enough to have had a leg or an arm shot off or to have been paralyzed. For the hero who had had his nerves all shot to pieces there were no such spontaneous tributes.

And that was the way it had always been with Tom Slade. He had always made good, but somehow, the applause and the grateful tributes had gone to others. Nature had not made him prepossessing and he did not know how to talk; he was just slow and dogged and stolid, like a British tank, as I said, and just about as homely. You could hardly expect a girl to make much fuss over a young fellow who is like a British tank, when there are young fellows like shining machine guns, and soaring airplanes - to say nothing of poison gas.

And after two years of service in the thick of danger, with bombs and bullets flying all about him; after four months' detention in an enemy prison camp and six weeks of trench fever, to say nothing of frightful risks, stolidly ignored, in perilous secret missions, this young chunk of the old rock of Gibraltar had come home with his life, just because it had pleased God not to accept the proffer of it, and because Fritzie shot wild where Tom was concerned. He couldn't help coming back with his life - it wasn't his fault. It was just because he was the same old Lucky Luke, that's all.

That had been Roy Blakeley's name for him - Lucky Luke; and he had been known as Lucky Luke to all of his scout comrades.

You see it was this way: if Tom was going to win a scout award by finding a certain bird's nest in a certain tree, when he got to the place he would find that the tree had been chopped down. Once he was going to win the pathfinder's badge by trailing a burglar, and he trailed him seven miles through the woods and found that the burglar was his own good-for-nothing father. So he did not go back and claim the award. You see? Lucky Luke.

Once (oh, this happened several years before) he helped a boy in his patrol to become an Eagle Scout. It was the talk of Temple Camp how, one more merit badge (astronomy) and Will O'Connor would be an Eagle Scout and Tom Slade, leader of the Elks, would have the only Eagle Scout at Camp in his patrol. He didn't care so much about being an Eagle Scout himself, but he wanted Will O'Connor to be an Eagle Scout; he wanted to have an Eagle Scout in his patrol.

Then, just before Will O'Connor qualified for the Astronomy Badge, he went to live with his uncle in Cincinnati and the Buffalo Patrol of the Third Cincinnati Troop pretty soon had an Eagle Scout among their number, and the Cincinnati troop got its name into *Scouting* and *Boy's Life*. Lucky Luke!

It was characteristic of Tom Slade that he did not show any disappointment at this sequel of all his striving. Much less had he any jealousy, for he did not know there was such a word in the dictionary. He just started in again to make Bert McAlpin an Eagle Scout and when he had jammed Bert through all the stunts but two, Uncle Sam deliberately went into the war and Tom started off to work on a transport. So you see how it worked out; Connie Bennett, new leader of the Elks presently had an Eagle Scout in his patrol and Tom got himself torpedoed. Mind, I don't say that Uncle Sam went into the war just to spite Tom Slade. The point is that Tom Slade didn't get anything, except that he got torpedoed.

One thing he did win for himself as a scout and that was the Gold Cross for life saving, but he didn't know how to wear it, and it was Margaret Eillson who pinned it on for him properly. I think she had a sneaking liking for Tom.

Poor Tom, sometime or other in his stumbling career he had probably gotten out of the wrong side of his bed, or perhaps he was born on a Friday. That was what Roy and the scouts always said.

And so you see, here he was back from the big scrap with nothing to show for it but a case of shell-shock, and you don't have bandages or crutches for shell-shock. There was young Lieut. Rossie Bent who worked downstairs in the bank, who had come home with two fingers missing and all of the girls had fallen at his feet and Tom had had to salute him. But there was nothing missing about Tom - except his wits and his grip on himself, sometimes.

But no one noticed this particularly, unless it was Mr. Burton and Margaret Ellison, and certainly no one made a fuss over him on account of it. Why should anybody make a hero of a young fellow just because he is not quite sure of himself in crossing the street, and because his mouth twitches? Boy scouts are both observant and patriotic, but they could not see that there was anything *missing* about Tom. All they had noticed was that in resuming his duties at the office he had seemed to be drifting away from them - from the troop. And when he came on Friday nights, just to sit and hear Roy jolly Peewee and to enjoy their simple nonsense, they thought he was "different since he had come back from France" - perhaps just a little, you know, *uppish*.

It would have been a lucky thing for Tom, and for everybody concerned, if Mr. Ellsworth, scoutmaster, had been at home instead of away on a business trip; for he would have understood.

But of course, things couldn't have gone that way - not with Lucky Luke.

CHAPTER V

ABOUT SEEING A THING THROUGH

But there was one lucky thing that Tom had done, once upon a time. He had hit Pete Connegan plunk on the head with a rotten tomato.

That was before the war; oh, long, long before. It was a young war all by itself. It happened when Tom was a hoodlum and lived with his drunken father in Barrel Alley. And in that little affair Tom Slade made a stand. Filthy little hoodlum that he was, instead of running when Pete Connegan got down out of his truck and started after him, he turned and compressed his big mouth and stood there upon his two bare feet, waiting. It was Tom Slade all over - Barrel Alley or No Man's Land - *he didn't run.*

The slime of the tomato has long since been washed off Pete Connegan's face and the tomato is forgotten. But the way that Tom Slade stood there waiting - that meant something. It was worth all the rotten tomatoes in Schmitt's Grocery, where Tom had "acquired" that particular one.

"Phwat are ye standin' there for?" Pete had roared in righteous fury. Probably he thought that at least Tom might have paid him that tribute of respect of fleeing from his wrath.

"'Cause I ain't a goin' ter run, that's why," Tom had said.

Strange to relate, Pete Connegan did not kill him. For a moment he stood staring at his ragged assailant and then he said, "Be gorry, ye got some nerve, annyhow."

"If I done a thing I'd see it through, I would; I ain't scared," Tom had answered.

"If ye'll dance ye'll pay the fiddler, hey?" his victim had asked in undisguised admiration....

Oh well, it was all a long time ago and the only points worth remembering about it are that Tom Slade didn't run, that he was ready to see the thing through no matter if it left him sprawling in the gutter, and that he and the burly truck driver had thereafter been good friends. Now Tom was an ex-scout and a returned soldier and Pete was janitor of the big bank building.

He was sweeping off the walk in front of the bank as Tom passed in.

"Hello, Tommy boy," he said cheerily. "How are ye these days?"

"I'm pretty well," Tom said, in the dull matter-of-fact way that he had, "only I get mixed up sometimes and sometimes I forget."

"Phwill ye evver fergit how you soaked me with the tomater?" Pete asked, leaning on his broom.

"It wasn't hard, because I was standing so near," Tom said, always anxious to belittle his own skill.

"Yer got a mimory twenty miles long," Pete said, by way of discounting Tom's doubts of himself. "I'm thinkin' ye don't go round with the scout boys enough."

"I go Friday nights," Tom said.

"Fer why don't ye go up ter Blakeley's?"

"I don't know," Tom said.

"That kid is enough ter make annybody well," Pete said.

"His folks are rich," Tom said.

That was just it. He was an odd number among these boys and he knew it. Fond of them as he had always been, and proud to be among them, he had always been different, and he knew it. It was the difference between Barrel Alley and Terrace Hill. He knew it. It had not counted for so much when he had been a boy scout with them; good scouts that they were, they had taken care of that end of it. But, you see, he had gone away a scout and come back not only a soldier, but a young man, and he could not (even in his present great need) go to Roy's house, or Grove Bronson's house, or up to the big Bennett place on just the same familiar terms as before. They thought he didn't want to when in fact he didn't know how to.

"Phwen I hurd ye wuz in the war," Pete said, "I says ter meself, I says, 'that there lad'll make a stand.' I says it ter me ould woman. I says, says I, 'phwat he starts he'll finish if he has ter clane up the whole uv France.' That's phwat I said. I says if he makes a bull he'll turrn the whole wurrld upside down to straighten things out. I got yer number all roight, Tommy. Get along witcher upstairs and take the advice of Doctor Pete Connegan - get out amongst them kids more."

I dare say it was good advice, but the trouble was that Lucky Luke was probably born on a Friday, and there was no straightening *that* out.

As to whether he would turn the world upside down to straighten out some little error, perhaps Pete was right there, too. Roy Blakeley had once said that if Tom dropped his scout badge out of a ten-story window, he'd jump out after it.

Percy Keese Fitzhugh

Indeed that *would* have been something like Tom.

Anyway the saying was very much like Roy.

CHAPTER VI

"THE WOODS PROPERTY"

When Tom reached the office he took a few matters in to Mr. Burton.

"Well, how are things coming on?" his superior asked him cheerily. "Getting back in line, all right? This early spring weather ought to be a tonic to an old scout like you. Here - here's a reminder of spring and camping for you. Here's the deed for the woods property at last - a hundred and ninety acres more for Temple Camp. We'll be as big as New York pretty soon, when we get some of that timber down, and some new cabins up.

"I'm glad we got it," Tom said.

"Well, I should hope," Mr. Burton came back at him. "That's off the Archer farm, you know. Gift from Mr. Temple. Runs right up to the peak of the hill - see?"

Tom looked at the map of the new Temple Camp property, which almost doubled the size of the camp and at the deed which showed the latest generous act of the camp's benevolent founder.

"Next summer, if we have the price, we'll put up a couple of dozen new cabins on that hill and make a bid for troops from South Africa and China; what do you say? This should be put

Percy Keese Fitzhugh

in the safe and, let's see, here are some new applications - Michigan, Virginia - Temple Camp is getting some reputation in the land."

"I had an application from Ohio yesterday," Tom said; "a three-patrol troop. I gave them the cabins on the hill. They're a season troop."

Mr. Burton glanced suddenly at Tom, then began whistling and drumming his fingers on the desk. He seemed on the point of saying something in this connection, but all he did say was, "You find pleasure and relaxation in the work, Tom?"

"It's next to camping to be here," Tom said.

"Well, that's what I thought," Mr. Burton said encouragingly. "You must go slow and take it easy and pretty soon you'll be fit and trim."

"I got to thank you," Tom said with his characteristic blunt simplicity.

"I don't know what we should do in the spring rush without your familiar knowledge of the camp, Tom," Mr. Burton said.

"I think he thinks more of the office than he does of the scouts," Margaret ventured to observe. She was sitting alongside Mr. Burton's desk awaiting his leisure, and Tom was standing awkwardly close by.

"I suppose it's because they don't grow fast enough," Mr. Burton laughed; "they can't keep up with him. To my certain knowledge young Peewee, as they call him, hasn't grown a half an inch in two years. It isn't because he doesn't eat, either, because I observed him personally when I visited camp."

"Oh, he eats *terrifically*," Margaret said.

"I like the troop better than anything else," Tom said.

"Well, I guess that's right, Tom," Mr. Burton observed; "old friends are the best."

He gathered up an armful of papers and handed them to Tom who went about his duties.

The day was long and the routine work tedious. The typewriter machine rattled drowsily and continuously on, telling troops here and there that they could have camp accommodations on this or that date. Tom pored over the big map, jotting down assignments and stumblingly dictated brief letters which Miss Ellison's readier skill turned out in improved form.

He was sorry that it was not Friday so that he might go to troop meeting that night. It was only Tuesday and so there were three long, barren nights ahead of him, and to him they seemed like twenty nights. All the next day he worked, making a duplicate of the big map for use at the camp, but his fingers were not steady and the strain was hard upon his eyes. He went home (if a hall-room in a boarding house may be called home) with a splitting headache.

On Wednesday he worked on the map and made the last assignment of tent accommodations. Temple Camp was booked up for the season. It was going to be a lively summer up there, evidently. One troop was coming all the way from Idaho - to see Peewee Harris eat pie, perhaps. I can't think for what other reason they would have made such a journey.

"And *you* will live in the pavilion in all your glory, won't you?" Margaret teased him. "I suppose you'll be very proud to be assistant to Uncle Jeb. I don't suppose you'll notice poor *me* if I come up there."

"I'll take you for a row on the lake," Tom said. That was saying a good deal, for *him*.

On Thursday he sent an order for fifteen thousand wooden plates, which will give you an idea of how they eat at Temple

Camp. He attended to getting the licenses for the two launches and sent a letter up to old Uncle Jeb telling him to have a new springboard put up and notifying him that the woods property now belonged to the camp. It was a long slow day and a longer, slower night.

Once, and only once, since his return, he had tried the movies. The picture showed soldiers in the trenches and the jerky scenes and figures made his eyes ache and set his poor sick nerves on edge. Once he had *almost* asked Margaret if he might go over to East Bridgeboro and see her. He was glad when Friday morning came, and the day passed quickly and gayly, because of the troop meeting that night. He counted the hours until eight o'clock.

When at last he set out for the troop room he found that he had forgotten his scout badge and went back after it. He was particular always to wear this at meetings, because he wished to emphasize there, that he was still a scout. He was always forgetting something these days. It was one of the features of shell-shock. It was like a wound, only you could not *see* it....

CHAPTER VII

JUST NONSENSE

How should those scouts know that Tom Slade had been counting the days and hours, waiting for that Friday night? They were not mind readers. They knew that Tom Slade, big business man that he was, had much to occupy him.

And they too, had much to occupy them. For with the coming of Spring came preparations for the sojourn up to camp where they were wont to spent the month of August. At Temple Camp troops were ever coming and going and there were new faces each summer, but the Bridgeboro Troop was an institution there. It was because of his interest in this troop, and particularly in Tom's reformation, that Mr. John Temple of Bridgeboro, had founded the big camp in the Catskills. There was no such thing as favoritism there, of course, but it was natural enough that these boys, hailing from Mr. Temple's own town, where the business office of the camp was maintained, should enjoy a kind of prestige there. Their two chief exhibits (A and B) that is, Roy Blakeley and Peewee Harris strengthened this prestige somewhat, and their nonsense and banter were among the chief features of camp entertainment.

Temple Camp without P. Harris, some one had once said, would be like mince pie without any mince. And surely Peewee had no use for mince pie without any mince.

"Oh, look who's here!" Roy Blakeley shouted, as Tom quietly took a seat on the long bench, which always stood against the wall. "Tomasso, as I live! I thought you'd be down at the Opera House to-night."

"I don't care thirty cents about the movies," Tom said, soberly.

"You should say thirty-three cents, Tomasso," Roy shot back at him: "don't forget the three cents war tax."

"Are you going to play that geography game?" Tom asked hopefully.

"Posilutely," said Roy; "we'll start with me. Who discovered America? Ohio. Correct."

"What?" yelled Peewee.

"Columbus is in Ohio; it's the same thing - only different," said Roy; "you should worry. How about it, Tomasso?"

Tom was laughing already. It would have done Mr. Burton and Mr. Ellsworth good to see him.

"We were having a hot argument about the army, before you came in," Connie Bennett said. "Peewee claims the infantry is composed of infants...."

"Sure," Roy vociferated, "just the same as the quartermaster is the man who has charge of all the twenty-five cent pieces. Am I right, Lucky Luke? Hear what Lucky Luke says? I'm right. Correct."

"Who's going to boss the meeting to-night?" Doc Carson asked.

"How about you, Tom?" Grove Bronson inquired.

Tom smiled and shook his head. "I just like to watch you,"

said he.

"It's your job," Doc persisted, "as long as Mr. Ellsworth is away."

There was just the suggestion of an uncomfortable pause, while the scouts, or most of them, waited. For just a second even Roy became sober, looking inquiringly at Tom.

"I'd rather just watch you," Tom said, uneasily.

"He doesn't care anything about the scouts any more," Dorry Benton piped up.

"Since he's a magnet," Peewee shouted.

"You mean a magnate," Doc said.

"What difference does it make what I mean?" the irrepressible Peewee yelled.

"As long as you don't mean anything," Roy shouted. "Away dull care; let's get down to business. To-morrow is Saturday, there's no school."

"There's a school, only we don't go to it," Peewee shouted.

"For that take a slap on the wrist and repeat the scout law nineteen times backward," Roy said. "Who's going to boss this meeting?

"I won't let anybody boss me," Peewee yelled.

Roy vaulted upon the table, while the others crowded about, Tom all the while laughing silently. This was just what he liked.

"Owing to the absence of our beloved scoutmaster," Roy shouted, "and the sudden rise in the world of Tomasso Slade, alias Lucky Luke, alias Sherlock Nobody Holmes, and his unwillingness to run this show, because he saw General Pershing and is too chesty, I nominate for boss and vice-boss of this meeting, Blakeley and Harris, with a platform...."

"We don't need any platform," Peewee shouted; "haven't we got the table?"

"It's better to stand on the table than to stand on ceremonies," Dorry Benton vociferated.

"Sure, or to stand on our dignity like Tomasso Slade," Westy Martin shouted.

"Put away your hammer, stop knocking," Doc said. "Are we going to hike to-morrow or are we going to the city?"

"Answered in the affirmative," Roy said.

"Which are we going to do?" Peewee yelled.

"We are!" shouted Roy.

"Do we go to the city?" Doc asked seriously.

"Posilutely," said Roy; "that's why I'm asking who's boss of this meeting; so we can take up a collection."

"All right, go ahead and be boss as long as you're up there," Connie Bennett said, "only don't stand on the cake."

"Don't slip on the icing," Westy shouted.

"I'll slip on your neck if you don't shut up," Roy called. "If I'm boss, I'd like to have some silence."

"Don't look at me, *I* haven't got any," Peewee piped up.

"Thou never spak'st a truer word," Westy observed.

"I would like to have a large chunk of silence," said Roy; "enough to last for at least thirty seconds."

"You'd better ask General Slade," said Doc; "he's the only one that carries that article around with him."

"How about that, Tommy?" Wig Weigand asked pleasantly.

Tom smiled appreciatively, and seemed on the point of saying something, but he didn't.

There was one other scout, too, who made a specialty of silence in that hilarious Bedlam, and that was a gaunt, thin, little fellow with streaky hair and a pale face, who sat huddled up, apparently enjoying the banter, laughing with a bashful, silent laugh. He made no noise whatever, except when occasionally he coughed, and the others seemed content to let him enjoy himself in his own way. His eyes had a singular brightness, and when he laughed his white teeth and rather drawn mouth gave him almost a ghastly appearance. He seemed as much of an odd number as Tom himself, but not in the same way, for Tom was matter-of-fact and stolid, and this little gnome of a scout seemed all nerves and repressed excitement.

"Let's have a chunk of silence, Alf," Roy called to him.

"Go ahead," Doc shouted.

"If there's going to be a collection, let's get it over with," Westy put in.

Roy, standing on the table, continued:

"SCOUTS AND SCOUTLETS:

"Owing to the high cost of silence, which is as scarce as sugar at these meetings, I will only detain you a couple of minutes...."

"Don't step on the cake," Doc yelled.

"The object of this meeting is, to vote on whether we'll go into the city to-morrow and get some stuff we'll need up at camp.

"Artie has got a list of the things we need, and they add up to four dollars and twenty-two cents. If each fellow chips in a quarter, we'll have enough. Each fellow that wants to go has to pay his own railroad fare - Alf is going with me, so he should worry.

"I don't suppose that Marshall Slade will condescend and we should worry. If we're going up to camp on the first of August, we'll have to begin getting our stuff together - the sooner the quicker - keep still, I'm not through. We were all saying how numbers look funny on scout cabins - five, six, seven. It reminds you too much of school. Uncle Jeb said it would be a good idea for us to paint the pictures of our patrol animals on the doors and scratch off the numbers, because the way it is now, the cabins all look as if they had automobile licenses, and he said Daniel Boone would drop dead if he saw anything like that - Cabin B 26. *Good night!*"

"Daniel Boone is already dead!" shouted Peewee.

"Take a demerit and stay after school," Roy continued. "So I vote that we buy some paint and see if we can't paint the heads of our three patrol animals on the three cabins. Then we'll feel more like scouts and not so much like convicts. If we do that, it will be thirty cents each instead of twenty-five."

Before Roy was through speaking, a scout hat was going around and the goodly jingle of coins within it, testified to the troops' enthusiasm for what he had been saying. Tom dropped in three quarters, but no one noticed that. He seemed abstracted and unusually nervous. The hat was not passed to little Alfred McCord. Perhaps that was because he was mascot....

CHAPTER VIII

FIVE, SIX, AND SEVEN

Then Tom Slade stood up. Any one observing him carefully would have noticed that his hand which clung to the back of the bench moved nervously, but otherwise he seemed stolid and dull as usual. For just a second he breathed almost audibly and bit his lip, then he spoke. They listened, a kind of balm of soothing silence pervaded the room, because he spoke so seldom these days. They seemed ready enough to pay him the tribute of their attention when he really seemed to take an interest.

"I got to tell you something," he said, "and maybe you won't like it. Those three cabins are already taken by a troop in Ohio."

"Which three?" Westy Martin asked, apparently dumb-founded.

"Oh boy, suppose that was true!" Roy said, amused at the very thought of such a possibility.

"Which three?" Westy repeated, still apparently in some suspense.

"Tomasso has Westy's goat," Roy laughed.

"Look at the straight face he's keeping," Doc laughed, referring to Tom.

"I might as well tell you the truth," Tom said. "I forget things sometimes; maybe you don't understand. Maybe it was because I wasn't here last year - maybe. But I didn't stop to think about those numbers being your - our - numbers. Now I can remember. I assigned those cabins to a troop in Ohio. They wanted three that were kind of separate from the others and - and - I - I didn't remember."

He seemed a pathetic spectacle as he stood there facing them, jerking his head nervously in the interval of silence and staring amazement that followed. There was no joking about it and they knew it. It was not in Tom's nature to "jolly."

"What do you mean, assigned them?" Connie asked, utterly nonplussed. "You don't mean you gave our three cabins on the hill to another troop?"

"Yes, I did," Tom said weakly; "I remember now. I'm sorry."

For a moment no one spoke, then Dorry Benton said, "Do you mean that?"

"I got to admit I did," Tom said in his simple, blunt way.

"Well I'll be -" Roy began. Then suddenly, "You sober old grave digger," said he laughing; "you're kidding the life out of us and we don't know it. Let's see you laugh."

But Tom did not laugh. "I'm sorry, because they were the last three cabins," he said. "I don't know how I happened to do it. But you've got no right to misjudge me, you haven't; only yesterday I told Mr. Burton I liked the troop, you fellows, best -"

Roy Blakeley did not wait for him to finish; he threw the troop book on the table and stared at Tom in angry amazement. "All right," he said, "let it go at that. Now we know where you stand. Thanks, we're glad to know it," he added in a kind of contemptuous disgust. "Ever since you got back from France I knew you were sick and tired of us - I could see it. I knew you only came around to please Mr. Ellsworth. I knew you forgot all about the troop. But I didn't think you'd put one like that over on us, I'll be hanged if I did! You mean to tell me you didn't know those three cabins were ours, after we've had them every summer since the camp started? Mr. Burton will fix it -"

"He can't fix it," Tom said; "not now."

"And I suppose we'll have to take tent space," Connie put in. "Gee williger, that's one raw deal."

"But *you* won't have to take tent space, will you?" Roy asked. "You should worry about *us* - we're nothing but scouts - kids. We didn't go over to France and fight. We only stayed here and walked our legs off selling Liberty Bonds to keep you going. Gee whiz, I knew you were sick and tired of us, but I didn't think you'd hand us one like that."

"Don't get excited, Roy," Doc Carson urged.

"Who's excited?" Roy shouted. "A lot *he* has to worry about. He'll be sleeping on his nice metal bed in the pavilion - assistant camp manager - while we're bunking in tents if we're lucky enough to get any space. Don't talk to *me*! I could see this coming. I suppose the scoutmaster of that troop out in Ohio was a friend of his in France. We should worry. We can go on a hike in August. It's little Alf I'm thinking of mostly."

It was noticeable that Tom Slade said not a word. With him actions always spoke louder than words and he had no words to explain his actions.

"All I've got to say to *you*" said Roy turning suddenly upon him, "is that as long as you care so much more about scouts out west than you do about your own troop, you'd better stay away from here - that's all I've got to say."

"That's what I say, too," said Westy.

"Same here," Connie said; "Jiminies, after all we did for you, to put one over on us like that; I don't see what you want to come here for anyway."

"I - I haven't got any other place to go," said Tom with touching honesty; "it's kind of like a home -"

"Well, there's one other place and that's the street," said Roy. "We haven't got any place to go either, thanks to you. You're a nice one to be shouting home sweet home - you are."

With a trembling hand, Tom Slade reached for his hat and fingering it nervously, paused for just a moment, irresolute.

"I wouldn't stay if I'm not wanted," he said; "I'll say good night."

No one answered him, and he went forth into the night.

He had been put out of the tenement where he had once lived with his poor mother, he had been put out of school as a young boy, and he had been put out of the Public Library once; so he was not unaccustomed to being put out. Down near the station he climbed the steps of Wop Harry's lunch wagon and had a sandwich and a cup of coffee. Then he went home - if one might call it home....

CHAPTER IX

ROY'S NATURE

Roy Blakeley was a scout of the scouts, and no sooner had he got away from the atmosphere of resentment and disappointment which pervaded the troop room, then he began to feel sorry for what he had said. The picture of Tom picking up his hat and going forth into the night and to his poor home, lingered in Roy's mind and he lay awake half the night thinking of it.

He had no explanation of Tom's singular act, except the very plausible one that Tom had lost his former lively interest in the troop, even so much as to have forgotten about those three cabins to which they had always seemed to have a prior right; which had been like home to them in the summertime.

When you look through green glass everything is green, and now Roy thought he could remember many little instances of Tom's waning interest in the troop. Naturally enough, Roy thought, these scout games and preparations for camping seemed tame enough to one who had gone to France and fought in the trenches. Tom was older now, not only in years but in experience, and was it any wonder that his interest in "the kids" should be less keen?

And Roy was not going to let that break up the friendship. Loyal and generous as he was, he would not ask himself why Tom had done that thing; he would not let himself think

Percy Keese Fitzhugh

about it. He and the other scouts would get ready and go to camp, live in tents there, and have just as much fun.

So no longer blaming Tom, he now blamed himself, and the thing he blamed himself for most of all was his angry declaration that Tom was probably acquainted with the scoutmaster of that fortunate troop in Ohio. He knew that must have cut Tom, for in his heart he knew Tom's blunt sense of fairness. Whatever was the cause or reason of Tom's singular act it was not favoritism, Roy felt sure of that. He would have given anything not to have said those words. Lukewarm, thoughtless, Tom might be, but he was not disloyal. It was no new friendship, displacing these old friendships, which had caused Tom to do what he had done, Roy knew that well enough.

In the morning, unknown to any of the troop he went early to the bank building to wait for Tom there, and to tell him that he was sorry for the way he had spoken.

But everything went wrong that morning, the trails did not cross at the right places. Probably it was because Lucky Luke was concerned in the matter. The fact is that it being Saturday, a short and busy day, Tom had gone very early to the Temple Camp office and was already upstairs when Roy was waiting patiently down at the main door.

CHAPTER X

TOM RECEIVES A SURPRISE

When Tom reached the office, he found among the Temple Camp letters, one addressed to him personally. It was postmarked Dansburg, Ohio, and he opened it with some curiosity, for the former letters in this correspondence had been addressed to Mr. Burton, as manager. His curiosity turned to surprise as he read,

DEAR MR. SLADE,

In one of the little circulars of Temple Camp which you sent us, your name appears as assistant to Mr. Burton in the Temple Camp office.

I am wondering whether you can be the same Tom Slade who was in the Motorcycle Corps in France? If so, perhaps you will remember the soldier who spent the night with you in a shell-hole near Epernay. Do you remember showing me the Gold Cross and saying that you had won it while a scout in America? I think you said you had been in some Jersey Troop.

If you are the same Tom Slade, then congratulations to you for getting home safely, and I will promise my scouts that they will have the chance this summer of meeting the gamest boy on the west front. I suppose you will be up at the camp yourself.

Send me a line and let me know if you're the young fellow whose arm I bandaged up. I'm thinking the world isn't so big after all.

Best wishes to you,

WILLIAM BARNARD,

Scoutmaster 1st Dansburg Troop, B.S.A.,
Dansburg, Ohio.

Tom could hardly believe his eyes as he read the letter. William Barnard! He had never known that fellow's name, but he knew that the soldier who had bandaged his arm (whatever his name was) had saved his life. Would he ever forget the long night spent in that dank, dark shell-hole? Would he ever forget that chance companion in peril, who had nursed him and cheered him all through that endless night? He could smell the damp earth again and the pungent atmosphere of gunpowder which permeated the place and almost suffocated him. Directly over the shell-hole a great British tank had stopped and been deserted, locking them in as in a dungeon. And when he had recovered from the fumes, he had heard a voice speaking to him and asking him if he was much hurt.

William Barnard!

And he had given the three cabins on the hill to Scoutmaster Barnard's troop in Dansburg, Ohio.

No one but Tom had arrived at the office and for just a few moments, standing there near Miss Ellison's typewriter and with the prosy letter files about, he was again in France. He could hear the booming of the great guns again, see the flashes of fire....

He sat down and wrote,

DEAR MR. BARNARD,

I got your letter and I am the same Tom Slade. I was going to ask you where you lived in America so I could know you some more when we got back, but when the doctors came to take me away, I didn't see you anywhere. I had to stay in the hospital three weeks, but it wasn't on account of my arm, because that wasn't so bad. It was the shell-shock that was bad - it makes you forget things even after you get better.

I was sorry early this morning that I gave you those cabins, because they're the same ones that my own troop always used to have, and it was a crazy thing for me to forget about that. But now I'm glad, because I have thought of another scheme. I thought of it while I was lying in bed last night and couldn't sleep. So now I'm glad you have those cabins. And you bet I'm glad you wrote to me. It's funny how things happen.

Maybe you'll remember how I thought I was going to die in that hole, and you said how we could dig our way out with your helmet, because if a fellow *has* to do something he can do it. I'm glad you said that, because I thought about it last night. And thinking of that made me decide I would do something.

I would like it if you will write to me again before summer, and you can send your letters care of Temple Camp, Black Lake.

When you come, you bet I'll be glad to see you.

Your friend,

TOM SLADE.

When Tom had sealed and stamped this letter, he laid the other one on Miss Margaret Ellison's desk, thinking that she might be interested to read it.

CHAPTER XI

TOM AND ROY

Anxious that his letter should go as soon as possible, Tom went down in the elevator and was about to cross the street and post it when he ran plunk into Roy, who was waiting on the steps.

"Good night, look who's here," Roy said, in his usual friendly tone; "I might have known that you were upstairs. You've got the early bird turning green with envy."

"I always come early Saturdays," Tom said.

"I want to tell you that I'm sorry about the way I spoke to you last night, Tom," Roy spoke up. "I see now that it wasn't so bad. I guess you have a whole lot to do up in the office, and maybe you just forgot about how we always had the hill cabins. You can't do *everything* you want to do, gee I realize that."

"I can do anything I want to do," Tom said.

Roy looked at him as if he did not quite understand.

"Going back on people isn't the way to square things," Tom said. "You got to make things right without anybody losing anything. There's always two ways, only you've got to find the other one."

Roy did not quite understand the drift of his friend's talk, it was not always easy to follow Tom, and indeed he did not care much what Tom meant; he just wanted him to know that their friendship had not been wrecked - could not be wrecked by any freakish act of Tom's.

"I don't care thirty cents what anybody says," Tom said; "I got to be fair."

"I'm not mad, you old grouch," Roy said, "and you should say sixty cents, because the price of everything is double. We should worry. I was waiting here to meet you so as to tell you that I don't know why you did that and I don't care. People have done crazier things than that, I should hope. We can bunk in tents, all right. So don't be sore, Tomasso. I'm sorry I said what I did and I know perfectly well that you just didn't think. You don't suppose I really meant that I thought you knew anybody in that troop out in Ohio, do you? I just said it because I was mad. Gee whiz, I know you wouldn't give anybody the choice before *us* - before your own fellows. I was mad because I was disappointed. But now I know how maybe you were all kind of - you know - rattled on account of being so busy."

"I ain't mad," said Tom, in his dull, stolid way; "I got to go across the street and mail this letter."

"And you'll come to meeting next Friday night?" Roy asked, anxiously.

"I don't know," Tom said.

"And I'm going to tell the fellows that you assigned five, six, and seven, to that Ohio troop just because you were thinking about something else when you did it, and that you didn't know anything more about those fellows than if they were the man in the moon," Roy paused a moment. "Did you?" he said conclusively.

"You can tell them whatever you want to," Tom said. "You can tell them that I didn't know anything about them if you want to. I don't care what you tell them."

Roy paused, hardly knowing what to say. In talking with Tom one had to get him right just as a wrestler must get his victim right and Roy knew that he must watch his step, so to speak.

"You can tell them they won't lose anything," Tom said.

"They'll lose something all right if they lose *you*, Tomasso," Roy said, with a note of deep feeling in his voice. "But we're not going to lose you, I can tell you that. They think you have no use for the scouts any more, because you met so many people in France, and know a lot of grown-up people."

"Is that what they think?" Tom asked.

They both stepped aside for Margaret Ellison, the Temple Camp stenographer, to pass in, and spoke pleasantly with her until she had entered the elevator.

"I don't care what they think," Roy said; "a scout is observant. Can't I see plain enough that you have your pioneer scout badge on? That shows you're thinking about the scouts."

"I put it on for a reason," said Tom.

"You bet your life you did," Roy said, "and it shows you're a scout. Once a scout, always a scout; you can't get away from that, Tomasso."

"Maybe you'll find that out," Tom said, his meaning, as usual, a little cloudy.

"I don't have to find it out, Tom," Roy said. "Don't you suppose I know where you stand? Do you think I'll ever forget how you and I hiked together, and how we camped up on my lawn together, when you first got to be a scout - do you think I will? I always liked you better than any fellow, gee whiz, that's sure. And I know you think more of us than you do of any one else, too. Don't you?"

"I got to go and mail this letter," Tom said.

"First you've got to say that you're for the scouts first, last and always," said Roy gayly, and standing in his friend's path.

Tom looked straight at him, his eyes glistening.

"Do you have to ask me that?" he said.

And then was when the trails went wrong, and didn't cross right and come out right. Roy went up in the elevator to get some circulars from Temple Camp office, and Tom, on his way back from across the street went into the bank to speak with Mr. Temple's secretary. And the girl spoiled everything, as Peewee Harris always said that girls are forever doing.

She was in a great hurry to get the cover off her machine and other matters straightened out, before Mr. Burton came in, so she did not trouble herself to talk much with Roy. She did, however, think to call after him just as he was leaving and he heard her words, with a kind of cold chill, as he stepped into the elevator.

She called to him in her sweetest tone, "Isn't it too funny! A scoutmaster, named Barnard, from out in Ohio who is going to be up at camp knew Tom in France. Won't they have a perfectly *scrumptious* vacation together, talking about old times?"

CHAPTER XII

THE LONG TRAIL

"You can tell them whatever you want to. You *can tell them that I didn't know anything about them* if you want to. I don't care what you tell them." These were the words that rang in Roy Blakeley's mind as he went down in the elevator, and they made him sick at heart. That Tom had so much forgotten about the troop, *his* troop, as to assign their three cabins to strangers - that Roy could overlook. He could not understand it, but in his fondness for Tom, he could overlook it, as his talk with Tom had proved.

But that Tom should lie to him and make him a party to that lie by authorizing him to repeat it, that he could not forget or forgive. "*You can tell them that I did not know anything about them if you want to.*" And all the while he, Tom, had known this Barnard, or whatever his name was, and had fixed things so that he and Barnard might be together at Temple Camp. Barnard was a grown-up fellow, Roy told himself, and a soldier, and he didn't exactly blame Tom, but....

And then their trails crossed again, right there at the foot of the elevator shaft, where Tom was waiting to go up.

Roy's first impulse was to brush past his friend saying nothing, but when he had all but reached the door he wheeled about and said, "If you want to hand out any lies to the troop, you'd better do it yourself; I'm not going to do it for you."

"What?" said Tom, a little startled out of his usual stolid manner.

"Oh, you know what, all right," Roy answered sneeringly. "You thought I'd never find out, didn't you? You didn't think I'd go up to the office. You thought you'd get away with it and have me lying to the troop - the fellows that used to be your friends before you met Barnyard or whatever you call him. I know who he is, all right. If you wanted to give him our cabins, him and his troop, why didn't you come and say so? Gee whiz, we would have been willing to do them a good turn. We've camped in tents before, if it comes to that."

Tom stood perfectly motionless, with no more expression, either of anger or sorrow or surprise, than he usually showed. His big, tight set, resolute mouth was very conspicuous, but Roy did not notice that. The elevator came down, and the metallic sound of its door opening was emphasized in the tense silence which followed Roy's tirade.

"Going up," the colored boy said.

The door rolled shut and still Tom Slade stood there, stolid and without any show of emotion, looking straight at Roy. "I didn't ever tell a lie - not since I got in with the scouts," he said simply.

"Well, that makes two," said Roy mercilessly; "do you mean to tell me you don't know what's-his-name - Barnard? Will you stand there and say you don't know him?"

"I do know him," Tom said; "he saved my life in France."

"And didn't you tell me only ten minutes ago that I could tell the fellows that you didn't know anything about - about that troop - about him and his troop? Didn't you? Do you deny that you did? You told me I could go back and lie to the fellows - you did! If you think I'll do that you've got another guess, I can tell you that much!"

"I never told you you should lie," said Tom with straight-forward simplicity, "and I admit I forgot about the cabins. I was away two summers. I had a lot of different things to think about. I got shell-shocked the very same night I met that fellow, and that's got something to do with it, maybe. But I wouldn't stand here, I wouldn't, and try to prove that I didn't tell a lie. If you want to think I did, go ahead and think so. And if the rest of the troop want to think so, let them do it. If anybody says I forgot about the scouts, he lies. And you can tell them they won't lose anything, either; you can tell them I said so. I ain't changed. Didn't I - didn't I ride my motorcycle all the way from Paris to the coast - through the floods - didn't I? Do you think it's going to be hard to make everything right? I - I can do anything - I can. And I didn't lie, either. You go up to Temple Camp on the first of August like you - like we - always did; that's all *I* say."

He was excited now, and his hand trembled, and Roy looked at him a bit puzzled, but he was neither softened nor convinced. "Didn't you as much as say you didn't know anything about who made that application - didn't you?" Roy demanded.

"I said it good and plain and you can go and tell them so, too," Tom said.

"And you do know this fellow named Barnard, don't you?"

"I know him and he saved my life," Tom said, "and if you -"

"Going up," the colored boy called again.

And the young fellow, scout and soldier, who would not bother to prove his truthfulness to his old companion and friend, was gone. He had hit his own trail in his own way, as he usually did; a long devious, difficult, lonesome trail. The clearly defined trail of the sidewalk leading to the troop room, where a few words of explanation might have straightened everything out, was not the trail for Tom Slade, scout. He would straighten things out another way. He would face this thing, not run away from it, just as he had set his big resolute mouth and faced Pete Connigan. They would lose nothing, these boys. Let them think what they might, they would lose nothing. To be falsely accused, what was that, provided these boys lost nothing? That was all that counted. What difference did it make if they thought he had lied and deceived them, so long as *he* knew that he had not?

And what a lot of fuss about three cabins! Had he not the power to straighten out his own mistake in the best possible way - the scout way? And how was that? By going to Mr. Burton and taking the matter up and perhaps causing disappointment to those boys out in Ohio, for the sake of these boys in Bridgeboro? Robbing Peter to pay Paul?

Perhaps Mr. Burton would have done that, under all the circumstances. Perhaps Mr. John Temple, head of the whole shebang, would have approved this - under the circumstances. Perhaps the average clerk would have proposed this; would have suggested hitting this convenient little trail, about as short and prosy as a back alley. All you need on that trail is a typewriter machine. Perhaps Tom Slade was not a good clerk. His way out of the difficulty was a longer and more circuitous way. But it was the scout way. He was a scout and he hit the long trail.

CHAPTER XIII

ROY'S TRAIL

As for Roy, he went home feeling heavy of heart, but he was not sorry for what he had said. He had known that Tom had been slipping away from the troop and that his interest in the old associations had waned ever since his return from France. But that Tom should have lied to him and that he should use Temple Camp and that old beloved spot up on the hill for new friends, deliberately giving them precedence over these companions of his real scouting days - *that* Roy could not stand. And he told himself that he was through with Tom, even as Tom was through with the troop.

The trail of Roy and his friends is short and easy to follow, and it is not the main trail of this story. It took them into the city where they bought a tent, (not a very large one, for they could not get together much money), but big enough to bunk in and enable them to spend their vacation at the beloved, familiar spot. He said that "he should worry about that fellow Barnard," and that he guessed Tom's fondness for that individual was like Peewee's fondness for mince pie - a case of love at first bite. But did he forget about Tom, and miss him at the meetings?

We shall have to guess as to that. Tom was seldom mentioned, at all events. The first member of the Bridgeboro troop to outgrow his companions and turn his thoughts to new friends and associates had broken away from the hallowed circle and deserted them, and repudiated them with a lie on his lips; that was what the scouts said, or at least, thought. They had seen it coming, but it had hurt just the same.

And so the days went by, and the breath of Spring grew heavier in the air, and the dandelions sprang up in the field down by the river, and tree blossoms littered the sidewalks, and the frogs began croaking in the marshes. When the frogs begin croaking it is time to think of camp.

But Tom Slade, late of the scouts, was ahead of the dandelions and the blossoms and the frogs, for on that very day of his talk with Roy, and while the three patrols were off on their shopping bee in the city, he went into Mr. Burton's private office and asked if he might talk to him about an idea he had.

"Surest thing you know, Tommy," said his superior cheerily. "You want to go to the North Pole now?"

For Mr. Burton knew Tom of old.

CHAPTER XIV

THE REALLY HARD PART

"Maybe you'll remember how you said this would just be a kind of an experiment, my starting to work again in the office, and maybe it would turn out to be better for me to go away in the country," said Tom.

"Yes sir," said Mr. Burton, with prompt good nature intended to put Tom at his ease.

"I was wondering if maybe you could keep a secret," Tom said.

"Well, I could make a stab at it," Mr. Burton said, laughing.

"Do you think Margaret could?" Tom asked.

"Oh, I dare say, but you know how girls are. What's the trouble?"

"I want to go away," Tom said; "I can't do things right and I want to go away. I'm all the time forgetting."

"I think you're doing fine," said Mr. Burton.

"I want to go up to Temple Camp until I feel better," Tom said.

Mr. Burton scrutinized him shrewdly and pursed up his lips

and said, "Don't feel first rate, eh?"

"I get rattled awful easy and I don't remember things," Tom said. "I want to go up to camp and stay all alone with Uncle Jeb, like you said I could if I wanted to."

Again Mr. Burton studied him thoughtfully, a little fearfully perhaps, and then he said, "Well, I think perhaps that would be a very good thing, Tom. You remember that's what I thought in the first place. You made your own choice. How about the secret?"

"It isn't anything much, only I thought of something to do while I'm up there. I got to square myself. I gave the troop cabins to a troop out west -"

"Well, I was wondering about that, my boy; but I didn't want to say anything. You'll have Roy and Peewee and those other gladiators sitting on your neck, aren't you afraid?"

"They got no use for me now," Tom said.

"Oh, nonsense. We'll straighten that out. You send a letter -"

"The scoutmaster of that troop out west is a friend of mine," said Tom, "but I never knew it until this morning, when I got a letter from him. They think I did it because I knew it was him all the time and liked him better, but I don't care what they think as long as nobody loses anything; that's all I care about. So if you'd be willing," he continued in his dull, matter-of-fact way, as if he were asking permission to go across the street, "I'd like to go up and stay at Temple Camp before the season opens and fell some of those trees on the new woods property and put up three cabins on the hill for Roy and the troop to use when they get there. I wouldn't want anybody to know I'm doing it."

"What?" said Mr. Burton.

"I want to go up there and stay and put up three cabins," said Tom dully.

"Humph," said Mr. Burton, sitting back and surveying him with amused and frank surprise. "How about the difficulties?"

"That's the only thing," Tom said; "I was thinking it all over, and the only difficulty I can think about is, would Margaret keep it a secret until the work is done, and you too. They think I'm not a scout any more, and I'm going to show them. If you think I can't do it, you ask Pete, the janitor. And if I straighten things out that way nobody'll get left, see? The hard part is really *your* part - keeping still and making her keep still."

"I see," said Mr. Burton, contemplating the stolid, almost expressionless face of Tom, and trying not to laugh outright.

"My part is easy," said Tom.

CHAPTER XV

A LETTER FROM BARNARD

When Tom reached Temple Camp he found a letter awaiting him there. It was stuck up among the antlers of Uncle Jeb's moose head which hung in the old camp manager's cabin. He found Uncle Jeb alone in his glory, and mighty glad to see him.

It was characteristic of the old western scout and trapper whom Mr. Temple had brought from Arizona, that he was never surprised at anything. If a grizzly bear had wandered into camp it would not have ruffled him in the least. He would have surveyed it with calm, shrewd deliberation, taken his corncob pipe out of his mouth, knocked the ashes out of it, and proceeded to business. If the grizzly bear had been one of the large fraternity who believe in "safety first" he would have withdrawn immediately upon the ominous sound of old Uncle Jeb's pipe knocking against the nearest hard substance. Uncle Jeb, like Uncle Sam, moved slowly but very surely.

It was not altogether uncommon for some nature loving pilgrim to drop in at camp out of season, and such a one was always sure of that easy-going western welcome. But if all the kings and emperors in the world (or such few of them as are left) had dropped in at camp, Uncle Jeb Rushmore would have eyed them keenly, puffed some awful smoke at them, and said, "Haow doo." He liked people, but he did not depend on them. The lake and the trees and the wild life talked to him, and as for human beings, he was always glad of their company.

It was also characteristic of Uncle Jeb that no adventurous enterprise, no foolhardy, daredevil scheme, ever caused him any astonishment. Mr. Burton, engrossed in a hundred and one matters of detail and routine had simply laughed at Tom's plan, and let him go to Temple Camp to discover its absurdity, and then benefit by the quiet life and fresh air. It would have been better if Tom had been sent up there long before. He had humored him by promising not to tell, and he was glad that this crazy notion about the cabins had given Tom the incentive to go. He had believed that Tom's unfortunate error could be made right by the romantic expedient of a postage stamp. Mr. Burton was not a scout. And Tom Slade was the queerest of all scouts.

So now Uncle Jeb removed his pipe from his mouth, and said, "Reckoned you'd make a trip up, hey?"

"I'm going to stay here alone with you until the season opens," Tom said; "I got shell-shocked. I ain't any good down there. I assigned our three cabins to a troop in Ohio. So I got to build three more and have 'em ready by August first. I'm going to build them on the hill."

"Yer ain't cal'latin' on trimming yer timbers much are yer?" Uncle Jeb asked, going straight to the practical aspects of Tom's plan.

"I'm going to put them up just like the temporary cabins were when the camp first opened," Tom said.

"Ye'll find some of them same logs under the pavilion," Uncle Jeb said; "enough for two cabins, mebbe. Why doan't you put up four and let that Peewee kid hev one all by hisself?"

"Do you think I can do it in six weeks?" Tom asked.

"I've seed a Injun stockade throwed up in three days," Uncle

Jeb answered. "Me'n General Custer threw up Fort Bendy in two nights; that wuz in Montanny. Th' Injuns thought we wuz gods from heaven. But we wuzn't no gods, as I told the general; leastways *I* was'n, n'never wuz. But I had a sharp axe.

"I knew I could do it," Tom said, "but I wanted it to be a stunt, as you might say."

"'Tain't no stunt," Uncle Jeb said. "Who's writin' yer from out in Ohio? I see the postmark. 'Tain't them kids from out Dayton way, I hope?"

Tom opened the letter and read aloud:

DEAR TOM,

When I save a fellow's life I claim the right to call him by his first name, even if I've never seen him. If anybody ever tells me again that the world is a big place, I'll tell them it's about the size of a shell-hole, no bigger, and that's small enough, as you and I know. All I can say is, "Well, well!" And you're the same Thomas Slade!

And the funny part of it is, we wouldn't know each other if we met in the street. That's because we met in a shell-hole. I tried to hunt you up along the line, made inquiries in the hospital at Rheims, and tried to get a line on you from the Red Cross and Y.M.C.A. Nothing doing. Somebody told me you were in the Flying Corps. I guess I must have fainted while they were taking you away. Anyway, when I woke up I was in a dressing station, trying to get my breath. I asked what became of you and nobody seemed to know. One said you were in the Messenger Service. When I left France I didn't even know you were alive.

And now you turn up in Temple Camp office and tell me to write you at Temple Camp. What are you doing up there before the season opens, anyway? I bet you're there for your health.

Do you know what I'm thinking of doing? I'm thinking of making a trip to camp and looking over our dug-outs and seeing what kind of a place you have, before I bring my scouts. How would that strike you? I've got three patrols and take it from me, they're a bigger job than winning the war. They're all crazy for August first to arrive.

Well, Tommy old boy, I'm glad I've met you at last. I have a hunch you're kind of tall, with gray eyes and curly hair. Am I right? I'm about medium height and very handsome. Hair red - to suggest the camp-fire.

I don't know whether my scouts will let me off for a week or two, but my boss wants me to take a good rest before I knuckle down to work. I'm off for August anyway. Don't expect me before that, but if I should show up on a surprise raid, don't drop dead. I may go over the top some fine day and drop in on you like a hand grenade. Are you there all alone?

Write me again and let's get acquainted. I'd send you a photo, only I gave my girl the last one I had.

So long,

BILLY BARNARD,
    Scoutmaster.

CHAPTER XVI

THE EPISODE IN FRANCE

Uncle Jeb smoked his pipe leisurely, listening to this letter. "Kind of a comic, hey?" he said. "I reckon ye'd like to hev 'em come. Hain't never seed each other, hey?"

Tom was silent. The letter meant more to him than Uncle Jeb imagined. It touched one of the springs of his simple, stolid nature, and his eyes glistened as he glanced over it again, drinking in its genial, friendly, familiar tone. So he had at least one friend after all. Cut of all that turmoil of war, with its dangers and sufferings, had come at least one friend. The bursting of that shell which had seemed to shake the earth, and which had shattered his nerves and lost him Roy and all those treasured friends and comrades of his boyhood, had at least brought him one true friend. He had never felt the need of a friend more than at that very moment. The cheery letter seemed for the moment, to wipe out the memory of Roy's last words to him, that he was a liar. And it aroused his memories of France.

"Maybe you might like to hear about it," he said to Uncle Jeb, in his simple way. "Kind of, now it makes me think about France. I wouldn't blame the scouts for not having any use for me - I wouldn't blame Roy - but anyway, it was that shell that did it. If you say so I'll start a camp-fire. That's what always makes me think about the scouts - camp-fire. Maybe you'll say I was to blame. Anyway, they won't lose anything. And when they come I'll go back home, if they want me to. That's only fair. Anyway, I like Temple Camp best of all."

"Kinder like home, Tommy," Uncle Jeb said.

The sun was going down beyond the hills across the lake and flickering up the water and casting a crimson glow upon the wooded summits. The empty cabins, and the boarded-up cooking shack, shone clear and sharp in the gathering twilight. High above, a great bird soared through the dusk, hastening to its home in the mountains, where Silver Fox trail wound its way up through the fastness, and where Tom and Roy had often gone. And the memory of all these fond associations gripped Tom now, and he had to tighten his big ugly mouth to keep it from showing any tremor of weakness.

"Maybe it won't be as easy as Uncle Jeb thinks," he said to himself, "but anyway, I'll be here and I won't be interfering with them, and I'll get the cabins finished and I'll go away before they come. They'll have to like Billy Barnard, that's sure; and maybe he'll tell them about my not knowing who he was until after I gave them the cabins. They'll all be on the hill together and they'll have to be friends...."

Yes, they would all be on the hill together, save one, and they would be friends and there would be some great times. They would all hike up the mountain trail, all save one, and see Devil's Pool up there. Tom hoped that Roy would surely show Barnard and his troop that interesting discovery which he and Roy had made. The hard part was already attended to - making Margaret and Mr. Burton keep still. And, as usual, Lucky Luke's part was the easiest part of all - just building three cabins and going away. It was a cinch.

"Shall I build a camp-fire?" he asked of Uncle Jeb.

And so, in the waning twilight, Tom Slade, liar and forgetter of his friends, built a camp-fire, on this first night of his lonely sojourn at Temple Camp. And he and Uncle Jeb sat by it as the night drew on apace, and it aroused fond memories in Tom, as only a camp-fire has the magic to do, and stilled his jangling nerves and made him happy.

"In about a month there'll be a hundred fellows sitting around one like this," he said.

"En that Peewee kid'll be trying to defend hisself agin Roay's nonsense," Uncle Jeb remarked.

"I ain't going to stay to be assistant camp manager this season," Tom said; "I'm going back to work. I'm having my vacation now. I kind of like being alone with you."

"What is them shell-holes?" Uncle Jeb asked. "Yer got catched into one, huh?"

And then, for the first time since Tom had returned from France, he was moved to tell the episode which he had never told the scouts, and which he had always recalled with agitation and horror. Perhaps the camp-fire and Uncle Jeb's quiet friendliness lulled him to repose and made him reminiscent. Perhaps it was the letter from Barnard.

"That's how I got shell-shocked," he repeated. "When you get shell-shocked it doesn't show like a wound. There's a place named Veronnes in France. A German airman fell near there. It was pretty near dark and it was raining, but anyhow I could just see him fall. I could see him falling down through the dark, like. I was on my way back to the billets for relief. I had to go through a marsh to get to that place where he fell. I thought I'd sink, but I didn't.

"When I got there I saw his machine was all crumbled up, and he was all mixed up with the wires and he was dead. I was going to give him first aid if he wasn't. But anyway, he was dead. So then I searched him and he had a lot of papers. Some of them were maps. I knew it wouldn't be any use to take them to billets, because the wires were all down on account of the rain. So I started through the marshes to get into the road to Rheims. Those marshes are worse than the ones we have here. Sometimes I had to swim. It took me two hours, I guess. Anyway, if you *have* to do a thing you can do it.

"When I got to the road it was easy. I knew that road went to Rheims because when I was in the Motorcycle Service I knew all the roads. Pretty soon I got to a place where a road crossed it and there were some soldiers coming along that road. I kept still and let them pass by and they didn't see me. I knew there were more coming and I could hear the sound of tanks coming, too. Maybe they were coming back from an attack.

"All of a sudden everything seemed bright and I saw a fellow right close to me and then there was a noise that made my ears ring and dirt flew in my face and I heard that fellow yell. As soon as I took a couple more steps I stumbled and fell into a place that was hot - the earth was hot, just like an oven. That was a new shell-hole I was in.

"I just lay there and my arm hurt and my ears buzzed and there was a funny kind of a pain in the back of my neck. That's how shell-shock begins. I heard that fellow say, 'Are you all right?' I couldn't speak because my throat was all trembling, like. But I could feel my sleeve was all wet and my arm throbbed. I heard him say, 'We must have had our fingers crossed.' Because you know how kids cross their fingers when they're playing tag, so no one can tag them? The way he says things in this letter sounds just like the way he said. He's happy-go-lucky, that fellow, I guess.

"There was a piece of the shell in there and it was red hot and by that he saw my arm was hurt, and he bandaged it with his shirt. He saw my scout badge that I wore and he asked me my name. That's all he knows about me. Pretty soon something that made a lot of noise moved right over the hole and I guess it got stuck there. He said it must be a tank that got kind of caught there. Pretty soon I could hardly breathe, but I could hear him hollering and banging with a stone or something up against that thing. I heard him say we could dig our way out with his helmet. Pretty soon I didn't know anything.

"The next thing I knew there was fresh air and people were carrying me on a stretcher. When I tried to call for that fellow it made me sob - that's the way it is when you're shell-shocked. You wring your hands, too. Even - even - now - if I hear a noise -"

Tom Slade broke down, and began wringing his hands, and his face which shone in the firelight was one of abject terror. And in another moment he was crying like a baby.

CHAPTER XVII

ON THE LONG TRAIL

That night he bunked in Uncle Jeb's cabin, and slept as he had not slept in many a night. In the morning his stolid, stoical nature reasserted itself, and he set about his task with dogged determination. Uncle Jeb watched him keenly and a little puzzled, and helped him some, but Tom seemed to prefer to work alone. The old man knew nothing of that frightful malady of the great war; his own calm, keen eyes bespoke a disciplined and iron nerve. But his kindly instinct told him to make no further reference to the war, and so Tom found in him a helpful and sympathetic companion. Here at last, so it seemed, was the medicine that poor Tom needed, and he looked forward to their meals, and the quiet chats beside their lonely camp-fire, with ever-growing pleasure and solace.

He hauled out from under the porch of the main pavilion the logs which had been saved from the fire that had all but devastated the camp during its first season, and saved himself much labor thereby. These he wheeled up the hill one by one in a wheelbarrow. There were enough of these logs to make one cabin, all but the roof, and part of another one.

When Tom had got out the scout pioneer badge which Roy had noticed on him, it had been by way of defying time and hardship and proclaiming his faith in himself and his indomitable power of accomplishment. As the work progressed it became a sort of mania with him; he was engrossed in it, he lived in it and for it. He would right his wrong to the troop by scout methods if he tore down the whole forest and killed himself. That was Tom Slade.

Up on the new woods property, which included the side of the hill away from the camp, he felled such trees as he needed, hauling them up to the summit by means of a block and falls, where he trimmed them and notched them, and rolled or pried them up into place. At times whole days would be spent on that further slope of the hillside and Uncle Jeb, busy with preparations for the first arrivals, could not see him at all, only hear the sound of his axe, and sometimes the pulleys creaking. He did not go down into camp for lunch as a rule, and spent but a few minutes eating the snack which he had brought with him.

At last there came a day when five cabins stood upon that isolated hilltop which overlooked the main body of the camp, and Tom Slade, leaning upon his axe like Daniel Boone, could look down over the more closely built area, with its more or less straight rows of cabins and shacks, and its modern pavilion. Five cabins where there had been only three. They made a pleasant, secluded little community up there, far removed from the hustle and bustle of camp life. "No wonder they like it up here," he mused; "the camp is getting to be sort of like a village. They'll have a lot of fun up here, those two troops, and it's a kind of a good turn how I bring them together. Nobody loses anything, this way."

True - nobody but Tom Slade. His hands were covered with blisters so that he must wind his handkerchief around one of them to ease the chafing of the axe handle. His hair was streaky and dishevelled and needed cutting, so that he looked not unlike one of those hardy pioneers of old. And now, with some of the rough material for the last cabin strewn about him and with but two weeks in which to finish the work, he was confronted with a new handicap. The old pain caused by the wound in his arm returned, and the crippled muscles rebelled against this excessive usage. Well, that was just a little obstacle in the long trail; he would put the burden on the other arm. "I'm glad I got two," he said.

He tried to calculate the remainder of the work in relation to the time he had to do it. For of one thing he was resolved, and that was to be finished and gone before those two troops arrived, the troop from the west and his own troop from Bridgeboro. They were to find these six cabins waiting for them. Everything would be all right....

He mopped his brow off, and rewound the handkerchief about his sore hand. The fingers smarted and tingled and he wriggled them to obtain a little relief from their cramped condition. He buttoned up his flannel shirt which he always left wide open when he worked, and laid his axe away in one of the old familiar cabins. It chanced to be one in which he and Roy had cut their initials, and he paused a moment and glanced wistfully at their boyish handiwork. Then he went down.

As he passed through Temple Lane he saw that Uncle Jeb had been busy taking down the board shutters from the main pavilion - ominous reminder of the fast approaching season. Soon scouts would be tumbling all over each other hereabouts. The springboard had been put in place at the lake's edge, too, and a couple of freshly painted rowboats were bobbing at the float, looking spick and glossy in the dying sunlight. Temple Camp was beginning to look natural and familiar.

"I reckon it'll be a lively season," Uncle Jeb said, glancing about after his own strenuous day's work. "Last summer most of the scouts was busy with war gardens and war work and 'twas a kind of off season as you might say. I cal'late they'll come in herds like buffaloes this summer."

"Every cabin is booked until Columbus Day," Tom said; "and all the tent space is assigned."

"Yer reckon to finish by August first?" Uncle Jeb asked.

"I'd like to finish before anybody comes," Tom said; "but I guess I can't do that. I'll get away before August first, that's sure. You have to be sure to see that 5, 6 and 7 go to my troop, and the new ones to the troop from Ohio. You can tell them it's a kind of a surprise if you want to. You don't need to tell 'em who did it. It's nice up there on that hill. It's a kind of a camp all by itself. Do you remember that woodchuck skin you gave Roy? It's hanging up there in the Silver Fox's cabin now."

"What's the matter with your hand?" Uncle Jeb inquired.

"It's just blistered and it tingles," Tom said. "It's from holding the axe."

CHAPTER XVIII

TOM LETS THE CAT OUT OF THE BAG

While they were having supper in Uncle Jeb's cabin, Tom hauled out of his trousers pocket a couple of very much folded and gather crumbled pieces of paper.

"Will you keep them for me?" he asked. "They're Liberty Bonds. They get all sweaty and crumpled in my pocket. They're worth a hundred dollars."

Mr. Burton had more than once suggested that Tom keep these precious mementos of his patriotism in the safe, but there was no place in all the world in which Tom had such abiding faith as his trouser side pockets, and he had never been able to appreciate the inappropriateness of the singular receptacle for such important documents. There, at least, he could feel them, and the magic feel of these badges of his wealth was better than lock and key.

"Keep them for me until I go away," he said.

Uncle Jeb straightened them out and placed them in his tin strong box.

"Yer ain't thinkin' uv stayin' on, then?" he queried.

"Not after I'm finished," Tom said.

"Mayn't change yer mind, huh?"

"I never change my mind," Tom said.

"I wuz thinkin' haow yer'd be lendin' me a hand," Uncle Jeb ventured.

"I'm going back to work," Tom said; "I had my vacation."

"'Tain't exactly much of a vacation."

"I feel better," Tom said.

Uncle Jeb understood Tom pretty well, and he did not try to argue with him.

"Be kinder lonesome back home in Bridgebory, huh? With all the boys up here?" he ventured.

"I'm going to buy a motor-boat," Tom confided to him, "and go out on the river a lot. A fellow I know will sell his for a hundred dollars. I'm going to buy it."

"Goin' ter go out in it all alone?"

"Maybe. I spent a lot of time alone. There's a girl I know that works in the office. Maybe she'll go out in it. Do you think she will?"

"Golly, it's hard sayin' what them critters'll do," Uncle Jeb said. "Take a she bear; you never can tell if she'll run for you or away from you."

Tom seemed to ponder on this shrewd observation.

"Best thing is ter stay up here whar yer sure yer welcome," the old man took occasion to advise him.

"One thing I'm sorry about," Tom said, "and that is that

Barnard didn't come. I guess I won't see him."

"He might come yet," Uncle Jeb said; "and he could give yer a hand."

"I'd let him," Tom said, "'cause I'm scared maybe I won't get finished now."

"I'm comin' up ter give yer a hand myself to-morrer," Uncle Jeb said, "and we'll see some chips fly, I reckon. Let's get the fire started."

Uncle Jeb was conscious of a little twinge of remorse that he had not helped his lonely visitor more, but his own duties had taken much of his time lately. He realized now the difficulties that Tom had encountered and surmounted, and he noticed with genuine sympathy that that dogged bulldog nature was beginning to be haunted with fears of not finishing the work in time.

Moreover, in that little talk, Tom had revealed, unwittingly, the two dominant thoughts that were in his mind. One was the hope, the anxiety, never expressed until now, that Barnard would come, and perhaps help him. He had been thinking of this and silently counting on it.

The other was his plan for buying a motor-boat, with his hundred or some odd precious dollars, and spending his lonely spare time in it, for the balance of the summer, back in Bridgeboro. He was going to ask a girl he knew, the *only* girl he knew, to go out in it. And he was doubtful whether she would go.

These, then, were his two big enterprises - finishing the third cabin and taking "that girl" out in the motor-boat which he would buy with his two Liberty Bonds. And away down deep in his heart he was haunted by doubts as to both enterprises. Perhaps he would not succeed. He still had his strong left arm, so far as the last cabin was concerned, and he could work until he fell in his tracks. But the girl was a new kind of an enterprise for poor Tom.

His plan went further than he had allowed any one to know.

Uncle Jeb, shrewd and gentle as he was saw all this and resolved that Tom's plans, crazy or not, should not go awry. He would do a little chopping and log hauling up on that hill next day. Old Uncle Jeb never missed his aim and when he fixed his eye on the target of August first, it meant business.

Then, the next morning, he was summoned by telegram to meet Mr. John Temple in New York and discuss plans for the woods property.

So there you are again - Lucky Luke.

CHAPTER XIX

THE SPECTRE OF DEFEAT

So Tom worked on alone. He made his headquarters on the hill now, seldom going down into the main body of the camp, and worked each day from sunrise until it was too dark to see. Then he would build himself a camp-fire and cook his simple meal of beans and coffee and toasted crackers, and turn in early.

Every log for this last cabin had to be felled and trimmed of its branches, and hauled singly up the hillside by means of the rope and pulleys. Then it had to be notched and rolled into place, which was not easy after the structure was two or three tiers high.

Building a log cabin is essentially a work for two. The logs which flanked the doorway and the window had to be cut to special lengths. The rough casings he made at night, after the more strenuous work of the day was done, and this labor he performed by the light of a single railroad lantern. The work of building the first two cabins had been largely that of fitting together timbers already cut, and adjusting old broken casings, but he was now in the midst of such a task as confronted the indomitable woodsmen of old and he strove on with dogged perseverance. Often, after a day's work which left him utterly exhausted and throbbing in every muscle, he saw only one more log in place, as the result of his laborious striving.

Thus a week passed, and almost two, and Jeb Rushmore did not return, and Tom knew that the next Saturday would bring the first arrivals. Not that he cared so much for that, but he did not see his way clear to finishing his task by the first of August, and the consciousness of impending defeat weighed heavily upon him. He must not be caught there with his saw and axe by the scouts who had repudiated him and who believed him a deserter and a liar.

He now worked late into the night; the straining of the taut ropes and the creaking of the pulleys might have been heard at the lake's edge as he applied the multiple power of leverage against some stubborn log and hauled it up the slope. Then he would notch and trim it, and in the morning, when his lame and throbbing arm was rested and his shoulder less sore after its night's respite, he would lift one end of it and then the other on his shoulder and so, with many unavailing trials finally get it lodged in place. He could not get comfortable when he slept at night, because of his sore shoulders. They tormented him with a kind of smarting anguish. And still Uncle Jeb did not return.

At last, one night, that indomitable spirit which had refused to recognize his ebbing strength, showed signs of giving way. He had been trying to raise a log into place and its pressure on his bruised shoulder caused him excruciating pain. He got his sleeping blanket out of the cabin which he occupied and laid it, folded, on his shoulder, but his weary frame gave way under the burden and he staggered and fell.

When he was able to pull himself together, he gathered a few shavings and built a little pyramid of sticks over them, and piling some larger pieces close by, kindled a blaze, then spreading his blanket on the ground, sat down and watched the mounting tongues of flame. Every bone in his body ached. He was too tired to eat, even to sleep; and he could find no comfort in the cabin bunk. Here, at least, were cheerfulness and warmth. He drew as close to the fire as was safe, for he fancied that the heat soothed the pain in his arm and shoulders. And the cheerful crackling of the blaze made the fire seem like a companion....

And then a strange thing happened.

CHAPTER XX

THE FRIEND IN NEED

Standing on the opposite side of the fire was a young fellow of about his own age, panting audibly, and smiling at him with an exceedingly companionable smile. In the light of the fire, Tom could see that his curly hair was so red that a brick would have seemed blue by comparison, and the freckles were as thick upon his pleasant face as stars in the quiet sky. Moreover, his eyes sparkled with a kind of dancing recklessness, and there was a winning familiarity about him that took even stolid Tom quite by storm.

The stranger wore a plaid cap and a mackinaw jacket, the fuzzy texture of which was liberally besprinkled with burrs, which he was plucking off one by one, and throwing into the fire in great good humor.

"I'm a human bramble bush," he said; "a few more of them and I'd be a nutmeg grater. I'm not conceited but I'm stuck up."

"I didn't see you until just this minute," Tom said; "or hear you either. I guess you didn't come by the road. I guess you must have come by the woods trail to get all those burrs on you."

For just a moment the stranger seemed a trifle taken aback, but he quickly regained his composure and said, "I came in through the stage entrance, I guess. I can see you're an A-1 scout, good at observing and deducing and all that. I bet you can't guess who I am."

"I bet I can," said Tom, soberly accepting the challenge; "you're William Barnard. And I'm glad you're here, too."

"Right the first time," said the stranger. "And you're Thomas Slade. At last we have met, as the villain says in the movies. You all alone? Here, let's get a squint at your mug," he added, sitting on the blanket and holding Tom's chin up so as to obtain a good view of his face.

Tom's wonted soberness dissolved under this familiar, friendly treatment, and he said with characteristic blunt frankness, "I'm glad you came. You're just like I thought you were. I hoped all the time that you'd come."

"*Get out!*" said Barnard, giving him a bantering push and laughing merrily. "I bet you never gave me a thought. Well, here I am, as large as life, larger in fact, and now that I'm here, what are you going to do with me? What's that; a light?" he added, glancing suddenly down to the main body of the camp.

"It's just the reflection of this fire in the lake," Tom said; "there isn't anybody but me in camp now. The season is late starting. I guess troops will start coming Saturday."

"Yes?" said his companion, rather interested, apparently. "Well, I don't suppose they'll bother us much if we stick up here. What are you doing, building a city? The last time we met was in a hole in the ground, hey? Buried alive; you remember that? Little old France!"

"I don't want to talk about that," Tom said; "when I told Uncle Jeb about it, it made me have a headache afterwards. I don't want to think about that any more. But I'm mighty glad to see you, and I hope you'll stay. It seems funny, kind of, doesn't it?"

Prompt to avail himself of Tom's apparent invitation to friendly intercourse, his companion lay flat on his back, clasped his hands over his head and said, "As funny as a circus. So here we are again, met once more like Stanley and Livingstone in South Africa. And do you know, you look just like I thought you'd look. I said to myself that Tom Slade has a big mouth - determined."

"I never thought how you'd look," Tom said soberly; "but I said you were happy-go-lucky, and I guess you are. I bet your scouts like you. Can you stay until they come?"

"They're a pack of wild Indians, but they think I'm the only baby in the cradle."

"I guess they're right," Tom said.

"So you're all alone in camp, hey? And making your headquarters up here? Nice and cosy, hey? Remote and secluded, eh? That's the stuff for me. I tell my scouts, 'Keep away from civilization.' The further back you get the better. Guess they won't bother you up here much, hey? Regular hermit's den. No, I'm just on a flying visit, that's all. Came to New York on biz, and thought I'd run up and give the place the once over. I might loaf around a week or two if you'll let me. Suppose I *could* stay until the kids get here, if it comes to that; *my* kids, I mean. After all it would be just a case of beating it back to Ohio and then beating it back here with them."

"You might as well stay here now you're here; I hope you will," Tom said. "As long as you're here I might as well tell you why *I'm* here, all alone."

"Health?"

"Kind of, but not exactly," Tom said. "These three cabins, the old ones - that one, and that one, and that one," he added, pointing, "are the ones my troop always had. But I forgot all about it and gave them to your troop. That got them sore at me. Maybe I could have fixed it for them, but that would have left you fellows without any cabins, because all the cabins down below are taken for August. So I came up here to build three more; that way, nobody'll get left. They don't know I'm doing it. I only got about two weeks now. I guess I can't finish because my arm is lame, on account of that wound - *you* know. And my shoulder is sore. I wanted to go away before they come - I got reasons."

His companion raised himself to a sitting posture, clasped his hands over his knees, and glanced about at the disordered scene which shone in the firelight. "So that's what you've been up to, hey?" he said.

"When I told you in my letter to address your letters here, that's what I was thinking about," Tom said. "Your troop and my - that other – troop will be good friends, I guess. I'm going home when I get through and I'm going to buy a motor-boat."

"Well - I'll - be - jiggered!" his friend said. "Thomas Slade, you're an old hickory-nut."

"It was just like two trails," Tom said, "and I hit the long one."

"And you're still in the bush, hey? Well, now you listen here. Can I bunk up here with you? All right-o. Then I'm yours for a finished job. Here's my hand. Over the top we go. On July thirty-first, the flag floats over this last cabin. I'm with you, strong as mustard. Building cabins is my favorite sport. You can sit and watch me. I'm here to finish that job with you - what do you say? Comrades to the death?"

"You can help," said Tom, smiling.

"That's me," said Billy Barnard.

CHAPTER XXI

TOM'S GUEST

Tom liked his new acquaintance immensely, but he did not altogether understand him. His apparently reckless and happy-go-lucky temperament and his breezy manner, were very attractive to sober Tom, but they seemed rather odd in a scoutmaster. However, he could think of no good reason why a scoutmaster should not have a reckless nature and a breezy manner. Perhaps, he thought, it would be well if more scoutmasters were like that. He thought that returned soldiers must make good scoutmasters. He suspected that scoutmasters out west must be different. Of one thing he felt certain, and that was that the scouts in William Barnard's troop must worship him. If he was different from some scoutmasters, perhaps this could be accounted for by the fact that he was younger. Tom suspected that here was just the kind of scoutmaster that the National Organization was after - one with pep. On the whole, he thought that William Barnard was a bully scoutmaster.

At all events he seemed to be pretty skillful at woodcraft. The next morning he set to work in real earnest and Tom took fresh hope and courage from his strenuous partner.

"This is *your* job," his friend would say; "all I'm doing is helping; sort of a silent partner, as you might say."

But for all that he worked like a slave, relieving Tom of the heavier work, and at night he was dog tired, as he admitted himself. Thus the work went on, and with the help of his new friend, Tom began to see light through the darkness. "We'll get her finished or bust a trace," Barnard said. They bunked together in one of the old cabins and Tom enjoyed the isolation and the pioneer character of their task. Relieved of the tremendous strain of lifting the logs alone, his shoulder regained some of its former strength and toughness, and the confidence of success in time cheered him no less than did the amusing and sprightly talk of his friend.

Barnard had not been there two days when his thoughtfulness relieved Tom of one of the daily tasks which had taken much time from his work. This was to follow the trail down the hillside and through the woods to where it ran into the public road and wait there for the mail wagon to pass and get the letters. "I'll take care of that," he said, as soon as Tom answered his inquiry as to how mail was received at camp, "don't you worry. I have to have my little hike every day."

There was quite an accumulation of mail when Uncle Jeb, looking strange and laughable in his civilized clothes, as Barnard called them, arrived on Saturday morning. The bus, which brought him up from Catskill, brought also the advance guard of the scout army that would shortly over-run the camp.

These dozen or so boys and Uncle Jeb strolled up to visit the camp on the hill, and Uncle Jeb, as usual, expressed no surprise at finding that Tom's visitor had come. "Glad ter see yer," he said; "yer seem like a couple of Robinson Crusoes up here. Glad ter see yer givin' Tommy a hand."

"I got a right to say he's my visitor, haven't I?" Tom asked, without any attempt at hinting. "'Cause I knew him, as you might say, over in France. We catch fish in the brook and we don't use the camp stores much."

"Wall, naow, I wouldn' call this bein' in the camp at all; not yet, leastways," Uncle Jeb said, including the stranger in his shrewd, friendly glance. "Tommy, here, is a privileged character, as the feller says. En your troop's coming later, hain't they? I reckon we won't put you down on the books. You jes stay here with Tommy till he gets his chore done. You're visitin' him ez I see it. Nobody's a goin' ter bother yer up here."

So there was one troublesome matter settled to Tom's satisfaction. He had wanted to consider Barnard as his particular guest on their hillside retreat and not as a pay guest at the camp. He was glad for what Uncle Jeb had said. But he was rather surprised that Barnard had not protested against this hospitality. What he was particularly surprised at, however, was a certain uneasiness which this scoutmaster from the west had shown in Uncle Jeb's presence. But it was nothing worth thinking about, certainly, and Tom ceased to think about it.

CHAPTER XXII

AN ACCIDENT

The time had now come when each day brought new arrivals to the camp, and August the first loomed large in the near future. It was less than a week off. The three new cabins stood all but completed, and thanks to the strenuous and unfailing help of his friend from the West, Tom knew that his scout dream of atonement was fulfilled.

"When they get here," he said to Uncle Jeb, "just tell them that they are to bunk in the cabins up on the hill. Barnard will be here to meet his own troop, and he'll take them up to the new cabins. Roy and the fellows will like Barnard, that's sure. It'll be like a kind of a little separate camp up on the hill; two troops - six patrols."

"En yer ain't a goin' ter change yer mind en stay, Tommy?"

"Nope," said Tom; "I don't want to see them. I'm going down Thursday. They'll all be here Saturday, I suppose."

In those last days of the work, little groups of scouts would stroll up from the main body of the camp to watch the progress of the labor, but the novelty of this form of entertainment soon passed, for the big camp had too many other attractions. In those days of hard work, Tom's liking for his friend had ripened into a feeling of admiring affection, which his stolid but generous nature was not slow to reveal, and he made the sprightly visitor his confidant.

One night - it might have been along about the middle of the week - they sprawled wearily near their camp-fire, chatting about the work and about Tom's future plans.

"One thing, I never could have finished it without you," Tom said, "and I'm glad you're going to stay, because you can be a kind of scoutmaster to both troops. I bet you'll be glad to see your own fellows. I bet you'll like Roy, too, and the other fellows I told you about. Peewee Harris - you'll laugh at him. He has everybody laughing. Their own scoutmaster, Mr. Ellsworth, is away, so it'll be good, as you might say, for them to have you. One thing I like about you, and that is you're not always talking about the law, and giving lectures and things like that. You're just like another fellow; you're different from a lot of scoutmasters. You're not always talking about the handbook and good turns and things."

His companion seemed a bit uncomfortable but he only laughed and said, "Actions speak louder than words, don't they, Tommy? We've *lived* it, and that's better, huh?"

"That's mostly the only thing that makes me wish I was going to stay," Tom said; "so's I'd know you better. I bet you'll keep those fellows on the jump; I bet you won't be all the time preaching to them. Mostly, the way my troop comes is across the lake. They hike up from Catskill through the woods. If your troop comes on the afternoon train, maybe both troops will come up through the woods together, hey? I'd like to see some of those scouts of yours. I bet they're crazy about you. You never told me much about them."

"We've been building cabins, Tommy, old boy."

"Yes, but now the work is nearly finished, all we have to do is clear up, and I'd like to hear something about your troop. Have they got many merit badges?"

"'Bout 'steen. Look here, Tommy boy; I think the best thing for you to do is to forget your grouch at Ray, or Roy, or whatever you call him, and just make up your mind to stay right here. This job you've done -"

"You mean *we*," Tom interrupted.

"Well, *we*, then - it's going to wipe out all hard feeling and everything is going to be all hunk. You'll make a better scoutmaster to the whole bunch than I will. I'm better at work than I am at discipline, Tom. I can't pull that moral suasion bunk at all. I'm pretty nifty at swinging an axe, but I'm weak on the good turn and duty stuff."

"You did *me* a good turn, all right," Tom said, with simple gratitude in his tone.

"But I mean the big brother stuff," his companion said; "I'm not so much of a dabster at that. You're the one for that - you're a scoutologist."

"A what?" Tom said.

"A scout specialist. One who has studied scoutology. You're the one to manage, what's-his-name, Peewee? And that other kid - Ray -"

"Roy," Tom corrected him.

"I was in hopes you'd weaken and decide to stay and we'd - they'd - elect you generalissimo of the allied troops, like old Foch."

Tom only shook his head. "I don't want to be here," he said; "I don't want to be here when they come. After they see the cabins you can tell them how I didn't know who you were until long after I - I made the mistake. They'll admit that this was the only thing for me to do; they'll admit it when they know about it. The only thing is, that I thought about it before they did, that's all. You got to admit it's the scout way, 'cause a scout wouldn't try to sneak out of anything the easy way."

"I don't know if it's the scout way," his companion said, "but it's the Tom Slade way."

"I got to be thankful I was a scout," Tom observed.

"I think the scouts have to be thankful," his friend said, with a note of admiration ringing in his voice.

"They thought I forgot how to be a scout," Tom said. "Now they'll see."

Barnard raised himself to a sitting posture, clasped his hands over his knees, in that attitude which had come to be characteristic of him about their lonely camp-fire, and glanced about at the results of Tom's long, strenuous, lonesome labors. And he thought how monotonous it must have been there for Tom through those long days and nights that he had spent alone on that isolated hilltop. As he glanced about him, the completed work loomed large and seemed like a monument to the indomitable will and prowess of this young fellow who seemed to him so simple and credulous - almost childlike in some ways. He wondered how Tom could ever have raised those upper logs into their places. It seemed to him that the trifling instance of thoughtlessness which was the cause of all this striving, was nothing at all, and in no way justified those weeks of wearisome labor. A queer fellow, he thought, was this Tom Slade. There was the work, all but finished, three new cabins standing alongside the other three, and all the disorder of choppings and bits of wood lying about.

He glanced at Tom Slade where he sat near him by the fire, and noticed the torn shirt, the hand wrapped in a bandage, the bruised spot on that plain, dogged face, where a chunk of wood had flown up and all but blinded him. He noticed that big mouth. The whimsical thought occurred to him that this young fellow's face was, itself, something like a knot of wood; strong and stubborn, and very plain and homely. And yet he was so easily imposed upon - not exactly that, perhaps, but he was simple withal, and trusting and credulous....

"If I get back before Saturday I can see that fellow," Tom said, "and buy his boat. He comes home early Saturday afternoons. He said I could have it for a hundred dollars if I wanted it. I got twenty-five dollars more than I need."

"You're rich. And the girl; don't forget *her*. She's worth more than a hundred and twenty-five."

"I'm going to give her a ride in it Sunday, maybe," Tom said.

For a few minutes neither spoke, and there was no sound but the crackling of the blaze and the distant voices of scouts down on the lake. "You can hear them plain up here," Tom said; "are your scouts fond of boating?"

Still his companion did not speak.

"Well, then," he finally said; "if you're going Thursday that means you go to-morrow. I was going to try to talk you into changing your mind, but just now, when I was piking around, and taking a squint at the work and at your face, I saw it wouldn't be any use. I guess people don't influence you much, hey?"

"Roy Blakeley influenced me a lot."

"Well then," said Barnard, "let's put the finishing touch on this job while both of us are here to do it. What do you say? Shall we haul up the flagpole?"

The shortest way down the hill in the direction of the new property was across a little gully over which they had laid a log. This was a convenient way of going when there was no burden to be borne. The hauling and carrying were done at a point some hundred feet from this hollow. In the woods beyond, they had cut and hewn a flagstaff and since two could easily carry it, Barnard's idea was that this should be done then, so that he might have Tom's assistance.

With Barnard, to think was to act, he was all impulse, and in two seconds he was on his feet and headed for their makeshift bridge across the gully. Tom followed him and was startled to see his friend go tumbling down into the hollow fully three feet from where the log lay. Before Tom reached the edge a scream, as of excruciating pain, arose, and he lost not a second in scrambling down into the chasm, where his companion lay upon the rocks, holding his forehead and groaning.

CHAPTER XXIII

FRIENDS

"Take your hand off your forehead," Tom said, trying gently to move it against the victim's will; "so I can tell if it's bad. Don't be scared, you're stunned that's all. It's cut, but it isn't bleeding much."

"I'm all right," Barnard said, trying to rise.

"Maybe you are," Tom said, "but safety first; lie still. Can you move your arms? Does your back hurt?"

"I don't want any doctor," Barnard said.

"See if you can - no, lie still; see if you can wiggle your fingers. I guess you're just cut, that's all. Here, let me put my handkerchief around it. You got off lucky."

"You don't call *that* lucky, do you?" Barnard asked. "My head aches like blazes."

"Sure it does," said Tom, feeling his friend's pulse, "but you're all right."

"I got a good bang in the head," said Barnard; "I'll be all right," he added, sitting up and gazing about him. "Case of look before you leap, hey? Do you know what I did?"

"You stepped on the shadow instead of the log," Tom said. "I was going to call to you, but I thought that as long as you're a scout you'd know about that. It was on account of the fire - the way it was shining. That's what they call a false ford -"

"Well, the next time I hope there'll be a Maxwell or a Packard there instead," Barnard said in his funny way.

"A false ford is a shadow across a hollow place," Tom said. "You see them mostly in the moonlight. Don't you remember how lots of fellows were fooled like that, trying to cross trenches. The Germans could make it look like a bridge where there wasn't any bridge - don't you remember?"

"*Some* engineers!" Barnard observed. "Ouch, but my head hurts! Going down, hey? I don't like those shadow bridges; it's all a matter of taste, I suppose. Oh boy, how my head aches!"

"If it was broken it wouldn't ache," said Tom consolingly, "or you wouldn't know it if it did. Can you get up?"

"I can't go up as quick as I came down," Barnard said, sitting there and holding his head in a way that made even sober Tom smile, "but I guess I can manage it."

He arose and Tom helped him through the gully to where it petered out, and so to their cabin. Barnard's ankle was strained somewhat, and he had an ugly cut on his forehead, which Tom cleansed and bandaged, and it being already late, the young man who had tried walking on a shadow decided that he would turn in and try the remedy of sleep on his throbbing head.

"Look here, Slady," he said, after he was settled for the night, "I've got your number, you old grouch. I know what it means when you get an idea in your old noddle, so please remember that I don't want any of that bunch from down below up here, and I don't want any doctor. See? You're not going to pull any of that stuff on me, are you? Just let me get a night's sleep and

I'll be all right. I'm not on exhibition. I don't want anybody up here piking around just because I took a double header into space. And I don't want any doctors from Leeds or Catskill up here, either. Get me?"

"If you get to sleep all right and don't have any fever, you won't need any doctor," Tom said; "and I won't go away till you're all right."

"You're as white as a snowstorm, Slady," his friend said. "I've had the time of my life here with you alone. And I'm going to wind up with you alone. No outsiders. Two's a company, three's a mob."

Something, he knew not what, impelled sober, impassive Tom to sit down for a few moments on the edge of the bunk where his friend lay.

"Red Cross nurse and wounded doughboy, hey?" his friend observed in that flippant manner which sometimes amused and sometimes annoyed Tom.

"I liked it, too, being here alone with you," Tom said, "even if it hadn't been for you helping me a lot, I would have liked it. I like you a whole lot. I knew I'd like you. I used to camp with Roy Blakeley up on his lawn and it reminded me of that, being up here alone with you. After I've gone, you'll mix up with the fellows down in the camp, but anyhow, you'll remember how we were up here alone together, I bet. You bet I'll remember that - I will."

Barnard reached out his hand from under the coverings and grasped Tom's hand. "You're all there, Tommy," he said. "And you won't remember how I got on your nerves, and how I tried walking on a shadow, and -"

Tom did not release his friend's hand, or perhaps it was Barnard who did not release Tom's. At all events, they remained in that attitude, hands clasped, for still a few moments more. "Only the *good* things about me, hey, Tommy boy?" his friend asked.

"I don't know any other kind of things," Tom said, "and if I heard any I wouldn't believe them. I always said your scouts must think a lot of you. I think you're different from other scoutmasters. You can *make* people like you, that's sure."

"Sure, eh?"

"It's sure with *me* anyway," Tom said.

"Resolution, determination, friendship - all *sure* with *you*. Hey, Tommy boy? Because you're built out of *rocks*. Bridges, they may be nothing but shadows, hey? According to you, you can't depend on half of them. I wonder if it's that way with friendships, huh?"

"It ain't with mine," Tom said simply.

And still Barnard clung to Tom's hand. "Maybe we'll test it some day, Slady old boy."

"There's no use testing a thing that's sure," Tom said.

"Yes?"

And still Barnard did not release his hand.'

"It's funny you didn't know about false fords," Tom said.

CHAPTER XXIV

TOM GOES ON AN ERRAND

Tom had intended to go down into camp for a strip of bandage and to see Uncle Jeb, but since Barnard was so averse to having his mishap known and to having visitors, he thought it better not to go down that night. He did not like the idea of not mentioning his friend's accident to the old camp manager. Tom had not been able to rid himself of a feeling that Uncle Jeb did not wholly approve of the sprightly Barnard. He had no good reason for any such supposition, but the feeling persisted. It made him uncomfortable when occasionally the keen-eyed old plainsman had strolled up to look things over, and he was always relieved when Uncle Jeb went away. Tom could not for the life of him, tell why he had this feeling, but he had it just the same.

So now, in order not to rouse his friend, who seemed at last to have dozed off, he lingered by the dying embers of their fire. As the last flickerings of the blaze subsided and the yellow fragments turned to gray, then black, it seemed to Tom as if this fire symbolized the petering out of that pleasant comradeship, now so close at hand. In his heart, he longed to wait there and continue this friendship and be with Roy and the others, as he had so often been at the big camp.

He had grown to admire and to like Barnard immensely. It was the liking born of gratitude and close association, but it was the liking, also, which the steady, dull, stolid nature is apt to feel for one who is light and vivacious. Barnard's way of talking, particularly his own brand of slang, was very captivating to sober Tom, who could do big things but not little things. He had told himself many times that Barnard's scouts "must be crazy about him." And Barnard had laughed and said, "They *must* be crazy if they like *me*...."

"He says I'm queer," Tom mused, "but he's queer, too, in a way. I guess a lot of people don't understand him. It's because he's happy-go-lucky. It's funny he didn't know about shadow bridges, because it's in the handbook." Then Tom couldn't remember whether it was in the handbook or not.... "Anyway, he's got the right idea about good turns," he reflected. "I met lots of scouts that never read the handbook; I met scoutmasters, too...."

And indeed there were few scouts, or scoutmasters either, who had followed the trail through the handbook with the dogged patience of Tom Slade. He had mastered scouting the same as he had mastered this job.

Barnard was pretty restive that night, tossed on his bunk, and complained much of his head aching. "It feels like an egg being beaten by an egg beater," he said; "I'm off the shadow bridge stuff for good and all. It throbs to the tune of *Over There*."

Tom thought this must be pretty bad - to throb to the tune of *Over There*. He had never had a headache like that.

"If you could only fall asleep," Tom said.

"Well, I guess I will; I'm pretty good at falling," his friend observed. "I fell for you, hey Slady? O-h-h! My head!"

"It's the same with me," said Tom.

"You got one too? *Good night!*"

"I mean about what you were saying - about falling for me. It's

Percy Keese Fitzhugh

the same with me."

"Same here, Slady; go to bed and get some sleep yourself."

It was two or three o'clock in the morning before the sufferer did get to sleep, and he slept correspondingly late. Tom knew that the headache must have stolen off and he felt sure that his companion would awaken refreshed. "I'll be glad because then I won't have to get the doctor," he said to himself. He wished to respect Bernard's smallest whim.

Tom did not sleep much himself, either, and he was up bright and early to anticipate his friend's waking. He tiptoed out of the cabin and quietly made himself a cup of coffee. It was one of those beautiful mornings, which are nowhere more beautiful than at Temple Camp. The soft breeze, wafting the pungent fragrance of pines, bore also up to that lonely hilltop the distant clatter of dishes and the voices of scouts from the camp below. The last patches of vapor were dissolving over the wood embowered lake, and one or two early canoes were already moving aimlessly upon its placid bosom. A shout and a laugh and a sudden splash, sounding faint in the distance, told him that some uninitiated new arrivals were diving from the springboard before breakfast. They would soon be checked in that pastime, Tom knew.

From the cooking shack where Chocolate Drop, the camp's famous cook, held autocratic sway and drove trespassing scouts away with a deadly frying pan, arose a graceful column of smoke which was carried away off over the wooded hills toward Leeds. Pretty soon Chocolate Drop would need *two* deadly frying pans, for Peewee Harris was coming.

Tom knew that nothing had been heard from the Bridgeboro scouts since Uncle Jeb had told him definitely that they were scheduled to arrive on the first, as usual. He knew that no other letter had come, because all the camp mail had passed through his hands. It had come to be the regular custom for Barnard to rise early and follow the secluded trail down to the state road where the mail wagon passed. He had early claimed it as his own job, and Tom, ever anxious to please him, had let him do this while he himself was gathering wood and preparing breakfast. "Always hike to work out west and can't get out of the habit," Barnard had said. "Like to hobnob with the early birds and first worms, and all that kind of stuff. Give me a lonesome trail and I'm happy - take one every morning before breakfast, and after retiring. How about that, old Doctor Slade?"

Old Doctor Slade had thought it was a good idea.

But this morning his friend was sleeping, and old Doctor Slade would not waken him. He tiptoed to the cabin and looked cautiously within. Barnard was sleeping the sleep of the righteous - to quote one of his own favorite terms. The bandage had slipped down from his forehead, and looked not unlike a scout scarf about his neck. A ray of early sunlight slanted through the crack between the logs and hit him plunk in the head, making his curly red hair shine like a red danger signal. He was sound asleep - dead to the wicked world - as he was himself fond of saying.

> Early to bed and early to rise,
> And you won't meet any regular guys.

As Tom paused, looking at him, he thought of that oft repeated admonition of his friend. He knew Barnard never meant that seriously. That was just the trouble - he was always saying things like that, and that was why people would never understand him and give him credit.... But Tom understood him, all right; that was what he told himself. "I got to laugh at him, that's sure," he said. Then he bethought him, and out of his simple, generous nature, he thought, "Didn't he say actions speak louder than words? That's what counts."

He tiptoed over to where that ray of sunlight came in, and hung his coat over the place. The shiny brightness of Barnard's hair faded, and the cabin was almost dark. Tom got his cap, and turning in the doorway to make sure his friend's sleep was undisturbed, picked his way carefully over the area of chips and twigs where most of the trimming had been done, and started down through the wooded hillside toward the trail which afforded a short-cut to the state road.

Once, and once only he paused, and that was to glance at a ragged hollow in the woods where a tree had been uprooted in some winter storm. It reminded him of the very day that Barnard had arrived, for it was after a discouraging afternoon with that stubborn old trunk that he had retraced his steps wearily to his lonesome camp and met the visitor who had assisted him and beguiled the lonesome days and nights for him ever since. Barnard, willing and ready, had sawed through that trunk the next morning. "Say nothing, but saw wood; that's the battle cry, Slady," he had cheerfully observed, mopping the perspiration from his brow.

And now, as Tom looked into that jagged hollow, his thoughts went even further back, and he thought how it was in some such earthen dungeon as this that he and Barnard had first seen each other - or rather, met. Barnard had thoughtfully refrained from talking of those things which were still so agitating and disturbing to poor Tom, but Tom thought of it now, because his stolid nature was pierced at last, and his heart was overflowing with gratitude to this new friend, who twice had come to his rescue - here on the isolated hillside on the edge of the beloved camp, and over there, in war torn France.

"You bet *I* understand him all right," said Tom. "Even if he talks a lot of crazy nonsense, he can't fool me. You bet *I* know what he is, all right. He can make believe, sort of, that he doesn't care much about anything. But he can't fool me - he can't."

CHAPTER XXV

TWO LETTERS

The trail wound its way through a pleasant stretch of woodland where the birds sang cheerily, and occasionally a squirrel paused and cocked its head in pert amazement at this rude intrusion into its domain. It crossed a little brook where Tom and Roy had fished many times, and groped for pollywogs and crawfish when Tom was a tenderfoot at Temple Camp. Those were happy days.

Where the trail came out into the state road there was a rough board across two little pedestals of logs, which the scouts of camp had put there, as a seat on which to wait for the ever welcome mail stage. The board was thick with carved initials, the handiwork of scouts who had come and gone, and among these Tom picked out R. B. and W. H. (which stood for Walter Harris for Peewee did not acknowledge officially his famous nickname). As Tom glanced at these crude reminders of his troop and former comrades, he noted wistfully how Peewee's initials were always cut unusually large and imposing, standing out boldly among others, as if to inform the observer that a giant had been at work. Everything about Peewee was tremendous - except his size.

Tom sat on this bench and waited. It reminded him of old times to be there. But he was not unhappy. He had followed the long trail, the trail which to his simple nature had seemed the right one, he had done the job which he had set out to do, they were going to have their three familiar cabins on the hill, and he was happy. He had renewed that strange, brief acquaintanceship in France, and found in his war-time friend, a new comrade. He felt better, his nerves were steady. The time had been well spent and he was happy. Perhaps it was only a stubborn whim, this going away now, but that was his nature and he could not change it.

When the mail wagon came along, its driver greeted him cheerily, for he remembered him well.

"Where's the other fellow?" he asked.

"I came instead, to-day," Tom said.

"That chap is a sketch, ain't he?" the man commented. "He ain't gone home, has he?"

"He's going to stay through August," Tom said; "his troop's coming Saturday."

"Purty lively young feller," the man said.

"He's happy-go-lucky," said Tom.

The man handed him a dozen or so letters and cards and a batch of papers, and drove on. Tom resumed his seat on the bench and looked them over. There was no doubt that Roy and the troop were coming; apparently they were coming in their usual manner, for there was a card from Roy to Uncle Jeb which said,

> Coming Saturday on afternoon train. Hope you can give us a tent away from the crowd. Tell Chocolate Drop to have wheat cakes Sunday morning. Peewee's appetite being sent ahead by express. Pay charges.

> So long, see you later.

P.S. Have hot biscuits, too.

ROY.

There were a couple of letters to Uncle Jeb from the camp office, and the rest were to scouts in camp whom Tom did not know, for he had made no acquaintances. There was one letter for Tom, bearing the postmark of Dansburg, Ohio, which he opened with curiosity and read with increasing consternation. It ran:

DEAR TOM SLADE,

I didn't get there after all, but now we're coming, the whole outfit, bag and baggage. I suppose you think I'm among the missing, not hearing from me all this time. But on Saturday I'll show you the finest troop of scouts this side of Mars. So kill the fatted calf for we're coming.

Slade, as sure as I'm writing you this letter, I started east, sumpty-sump days ago and was going to drop in on you and have a little visit, just we two, before this noisy bunch got a chance to interfere. We'll just have to sneak away from them and get off in the woods alone and talk about old times in France.

Maybe you won't believe it, but I got as far as Columbus and there was a telegram from my boss, "Come in, come in, wherever you are." Can you beat that? So back I went on the next train. You'll have to take the will for the deed, old man.

Don't you care; now I'm coming with my expeditionary forces, and you and I'll foil them yet. One of our office men was taken sick, that was the trouble. And I've been so busy doing his work and my own, and getting this crew of wild Indians ready to invade Temple Camp, that I haven't had time to write a letter, that's a fact. Even at this very minute, one young tenderfoot is shouting in my ear that he's crazy to see that fellow I bunked into in France. He says he thinks the troop you're mixed up with must think you're a great hero.

So bye bye, till I see you,

W. BARNARD.

Twice, three times, Tom read this letter through, in utter dismay. What did it mean? He squinted his eyes and scrutinized the signature, as if to make sure that he read it aright. There was the name, W. Barnard. The handwriting was Barnard's, too. And the envelope had been postmarked in Dansburg, Ohio, two days prior to the day of its arrival.

How could this be? What did it mean?

CHAPTER XXVI

LUCKY LUKE'S FRIEND

Tom returned through the woods in a kind of trance, pausing once to glance through the letter again and to scrutinize the signature. He found the patient up and about, with no reminder of his mishap save the cut on his forehead. He was plainly agitated and expectant as he looked through the woods and saw Tom coming. It was clear that he was in some suspense, but Tom, who would have noticed the smallest insect or most indistinct footprint in the path, did not observe this.

"H'lo, Slady," he said with a fine show of unconcern; "out for the early worm?" He did not fail to give a sidelong glance at Tom's pocket.

"Is your headache all gone?" Tom asked.

"Sneaked off just like you," he said; "I was wondering where you were. I see you were down for the mail. Anything doing?" he asked with ill-concealed curiosity.

"They're coming," Tom said.

"Who's coming?"

"Roy and the troop," Tom answered.

"Oh. Nothing important, huh?"

"I got some mail for camp; I'm going down to Uncle Jeb's cabin; I'll be right back," Tom said.

His friend looked at him curiously, anxiously, as Tom started down the hill.

"I won't make any breaks," Tom said simply, leaving his friend to make what he would of this remark. The other watched him for a moment and seemed satisfied.

Having delivered the mail without the smallest sign of discomposure, he tramped up the hill again in his customary plodding manner. His friend was sitting on the door sill of one of the new cabins, whittling a stick. He looked as if he might have been reflecting, as one is apt to do when whittling a stick.

"You got to tell me who you are?" Tom said, standing directly in front of him.

"You got a letter? I thought so," his friend said, quietly. "Sit down, Slady."

For just a moment Tom hesitated, then he sat down on the sill alongside his companion.

"All right, old man," said the other; "spring it - you're through with me for good?"

"You got to tell me who you are," Tom said doggedly; "first you got to tell me who you are."

For a few moments they sat there in silence, Tom's companion whittling the stick and pondering.

"I ain't mad, anyway," Tom finally said.

"You're not?" the other asked.

"It don't make any difference as long as you're my friend, and you helped me."

The other looked up at him in surprise, surveying Tom's stolid, almost expressionless face which was fixed upon the distant camp. "You're solid, fourteen karat gold, Slady," he finally said. "I'm bad enough, goodness knows; but to put it over on a fellow like you, just because you're easy, it's - it just makes me feel like - Oh, I don't know - like a sneak. I'm ashamed to look you in the face, Slady."

Still Tom said nothing, only looked off through the trees below, where specks of white could be seen here and there amid the foliage. "They're putting up the overflow tents," he said, irrelevantly; "there'll be a lot coming Saturday."

Then, again, there was silence for a few moments.

"I'm used to having things turn out different from the way I expected," Tom said, dully.

"Slady -" his friend began, but paused.

And for a few moments there was silence again, save for the distant sound of splashing down at the lake's edge, where scouts were swimming.

"Slady - listen, Slady; as sure as I sit here ... Are you listening, Slady? As sure as I sit here, I'm going to tell you the truth - every god darned last word of it."

"I never said you lied," Tom said, never looking at him.

"No? I tried not to tell many. But I've been *living* one; that's worse. I'm so contemptible I - it's putting anything over on *you* - that's what makes me feel such a contemptible, low down sneak. That's what's got me. I don't care so much about the other part. It's *you* - Slady -"

He put his hand on Tom's shoulder and looked at him with a kind of expectancy. And still Tom's gaze was fixed upon the camp below them.

"I don't mind having things go wrong," Tom said, with a kind of pathetic dullness that must have gone straight to the other's heart. "As long as I got a friend it doesn't make any difference what one - I mean who he is. Lots of times the wrong trail takes you to a better place."

"Do you know where it's taking you *this* time? It isn't a question of *who* I am. It's a question of *what* I am - Slady. Do you know what I am?"

"You're a friend of mine," Tom said.

His companion slowly drew his hand from Tom's shoulder, and gazed, perplexed and dumfounded, into that square, homely, unimpassioned face.

"I'm a thief, Slady," he said.

"I used to steal things," Tom said.

CHAPTER XXVII

THORNTON'S STORY

It was very much like Tom Slade that this altogether sensational disclosure and startling announcement did not greatly agitate him, nor even make him especially curious. The fact that this seductive stranger was his friend seemed the one outstanding reality to him. If he had any other feelings, of humiliation at being so completely deceived, or of disappointment, he did not show them. But he did reiterate in that dull way of his, "You got to tell me who you are."

"I'm *going* to tell, Slady," his friend said, with a note of sincerity there was no mistaking; "I'm going to tell you the whole business. What did *you* ever steal? An apple out of a grocery store, or something like that? I thought so. You wouldn't know how to steal if you tried; you'd make a bungle of it."

"That's the way I do, sometimes," Tom said.

"Is it? Well, you didn't this time - old man. If I'm your friend, I'm going to be worth it. Do you get that?"

"I told you you was."

"Slady, I never knew what I was going to get up against, or I would never have tried to swing this thing. If you'd turned out to be a different kind of a fellow I wouldn't have felt so much like a sneak. It's *you* that makes me feel like a criminal - not those sleuths and bloodhounds out there. Listen, Slady; it's a kind of a camp-fire story, as you would call it, that I'm going to tell you."

He laid his hand on Tom's arm as he talked and so they sat there on the rough sill of the cabin doorway, Tom silent, the other eager, anxious, as he related his story. The birds flitted about and chirped in the trees overhead, busy with their morning games or tasks, and below the voices of scouts could be heard, thin and spent by the distance, and occasionally the faint sound of a diver with accompanying shouts and laughter which Tom seemed to hear as in a dream. Far off, beyond the mountains, could be heard the shrill whistle of a train, bringing scouts, perhaps, to crowd the already filled tent space. And amid all these distant sounds which, subdued, formed a kind of outdoor harmony, the voice of Tom's companion sounded strangely in his ear.

"My home is out in Broadvale, Ohio, Slady. Ever hear of it? It's west of Dansburg - about fifty miles. I worked in a lumber concern out there. Can you guess the rest? Here's what did it, Slady, (and with admirable dexterity he went through the motions of shuffling cards and shooting craps). I swiped a hundred, Slady. Don't ask me why I did it - I don't know - I was crazy, that's all. So *now* what have you got to say?" he inquired with a kind of recklessness, releasing Tom's arm.

"I ain't got anything to say," said Tom.

"They don't know it yet, Tommy, but they'll know it Monday. The accountants are on the job Monday. So I beat it, while the going was good. I started east, for little old New York. I intended to change my name and get a job there and lay low till I could make good. I thought they'd never find me in New York. My right name is Thornton, Slady. Red Thornton they call me out home, on account of this brick dome. Tommy, old boy, as sure as you sit there I don't know any more about the boy scouts than a pig knows about hygiene. So now you've got my number, Slady. What is it? Quits?"

"If you knew anything about scouts," Tom said, with the faintest note of huskiness in his voice, "you'd know that they don't call quits. If I was a quitter, do you suppose I'd have stuck up here?"

Thornton gazed about him at the three new cabins, which this queer friend of his had built there to rectify a trifling act of forgetfulness; he looked at Tom's torn shirt, through which his bruised shoulder could be seen, and at those tough scarred hands.

"So now you know something about them," Tom said.

"I know something about *one* of them, anyway," Thornton replied admiringly.

"If a fellow sticks in one way, he'll stick in another way," Tom said. "If he makes up his mind to a thing -"

"You said it, Slady," Thornton concurred, giving Tom a rap on the shoulder. "And now you know, you won't tell? You won't tell that I've gone to New York?" he added with sudden anxiety.

"Who would I tell?" Tom asked. "Nobody ever made me do anything yet that I didn't want to do." Which was only too true.

Thornton crossed one knee over the other and talked with more ease and assurance. "I met Barnard on the train coming east, Slady. He has red hair like mine, so I thought I'd sit down beside him; we harmonized."

Tom could not repress a smile. "He told me in a letter that he had red hair," he observed.

"Red as a Temple Camp sunset, Tommy old boy. You're going to like that fellow; he's a hundred per cent, white - only for his hair. He's got scouting on the brain - clean daft about it. He told me all about you and how he and his crew of kids were going to spend August here and make things lively. Your crowd -"

"Troop," Tom said.

"Right-o; your troop had better look out for that bunch - excuse me, *troop*. Right? I'm learning, hey? I'll be a good scout when I get out of jail," he added soberly. "Never mind; listen. Barnard thinks you're the only scout outside of Dansburg, Ohio. He told me how he was coming here to give you a little surprise call before the season opened and the kids - guys - scouts, right-o, began coming. Tom," he added seriously, "by the time we got to Columbus, I knew as much about Temple Camp and you, as *he* did. He didn't know so much about *you* either, if it comes to that. But I found out that you were pretty nearly all alone here.

"Then he got a wire, Tom; I think it was in Columbus. A brakeman came through the train with a message, calling his name. Oh, boy, but he was piffed! 'Got to go home,' he said. That's all there was to it, Tom. Business before pleasure, hey? Poor fellow, I felt sorry for him. He found out he could get a train back in about an hour.

"Tommy, listen here. It wasn't until my train started and I looked back and waved to him out of the window, that this low down game I've put over on you occurred to me. All the time that we were chatting together, I was worried, thinking about what I'd do and where I'd go, and how it would be on the first Monday in August when those pen and ink sleuths got the goods on me. I could just see them going over my ledger, Slady.

"Well, I looked out of the car window and there stood Barnard, and the sun was just going down, Tommy, just like you and I have watched it do night after night up here, and that red hair of his was just shining in the light. It came to me just like that, Slady," Thornton said, clapping his hands, "and I said to myself, I'm like that chap in *one* way, anyhow, and he and this fellow Slade have *never seen each other*. Why can't *I* go up to that lonely camp in the mountains and be Billy Barnard for a while? Why can't I lie low there till I can plan what to do next? That's what I said, Slady. Wouldn't a place like that be better than New York? Maybe you'll say I took a long chance - reckless. That's the way it is with red hair, Slady. I took a chance on you being easy and it worked out, that's all. Or rather, I mean it *didn't*, for I feel like a murderer, and it's all on account of you, Slady.

"I didn't know what to do, I didn't know where to go; I just wanted to get away from home before the game was up and they nabbed me. It's no fun being pinched, Tom. I thought I might make the visit that this friend of yours was going to make, and hang around here where it's quiet and lonesome, till it was time for him to come. I guess that's about as far as my plans carried. It was a crazy idea, I see that well enough now. But I was rattled - I was just rattled, that's all. I thought that when the time came that I'd have to leave here, maybe I could tramp up north further and change my name again and get a job on some farm or other, till I could earn a little and make good. What I didn't figure on was the kind of a fellow I was going to meet. I - I -" he stammered, trying to control himself in a burst of feeling and clutching Tom's knee, "I - I didn't put it over on you, Tom; maybe it seems that way to you - but - but I didn't. It's you that win, old man - can't you see? It's *you* that win. You've put it all over *me* and rubbed it in, and - and - instead of getting away with anything - like I thought - I'll just beat it away from here feeling like a bigger sneak than I ever thought I was. I've - I've seen something here - I have. I thought some of these trees were made of pretty good stuff, but you've got them beat, Slady. I thought I was a wise guy to dig into this forsaken retreat and slip the bandage over your eyes, but - but the laugh is on me, Slady, don't - don't you see?" he smiled, his eyes glistening and his hand trembling on

Tom's knee. "You've put it all over me, you old hickory-nut, and I've told you the whole business, and you've got me in your power, see?"

Tom Slade looked straight ahead of him and said never a word.

"It's - it's a knockout, Slady, and you win. You can go down and tell old Uncle Jeb the whole business," he fairly sobbed, "I won't stop you. I'm sick and discouraged - I might as well take my medicine - I'm - I'm sick of the whole thing - you win - Slady. I'll wait here - I - I won't fool you again - not once again, by thunder, I won't! Go on down and tell him a thief has been bunking up here with you - go on - I'll wait."

There was just a moment of silence, and in that moment, strangely enough, a merry laugh arose in the camp below.

"You needn't tell me what to do," said Tom, "because I *know* what to do. There's nobody in this world can tell me what to do. Mr. Burton, he wanted to write to those fellows and fix it. But I knew what to do. Do you call me a quitter? You see these cabins, don't you? Do you think *you* can tell me what to do?"

"Go and send a wire to Broadvale and tell 'em that you've got me," Thornton said with a kind of bitter resignation; "I heard that scouts are good at finding missing people - fugitives. You - you *have got* me, Tommy, but in a different way than you think. You got me that first night. Go ahead. But - but listen here. I *can't* let them take me to-day, my head is spinning like a buzz-saw, Tommy - I can't, I can't, I *can't*! It's the cut in my head. All this starts it aching again - it just - "

He lowered his head until his wounded forehead rested on Tom's lap. "I'm - I'm just - beaten," he sobbed. "Let me stay here to-day, to-night - don't say anything yet - let me stay just this one day more with you and to-morrow I'll be better and you can go down and tell. I won't run away - don't you believe me? I'll take what's coming to me. Only wait - my head is all buzzing again now - just wait till to-morrow. Let me stay here to-day, old man ..."

Tom Slade lifted the head from his lap and arose. "You can't stay here to-night," he said; "you can't stay even to-day. You can't stay an hour. Nobody can tell me what I ought to do. You can't stay here ten minutes. If you tried to get away I'd trail you, I'd catch you. You stay where you are till I get back."

CHAPTER XXVIII

RED THORNTON LEARNS
SOMETHING ABOUT SCOUTS

And strange to say Red Thornton did stay just where he was. Perhaps, seeing that Tom limped as he went down the hill, the fugitive entertained a momentary thought of flight. If so, he abandoned it, perhaps in fear, more likely in honor. Who shall say? His agitation had caused his head to begin aching furiously again, and he was a pitiful figure as he sat there upon the doorsill, in a kind of desperate resignation, resting his forehead in his two hands, and occasionally looking along the path down the hill at Tom as he limped in and out among the trees, following the beaten trail. It had never occurred to him before, how lame Tom was, as the result of his injuries and excessive labors. And he marvelled at the simple confidence which would leave him thus free to escape, if he cared to. Perhaps Tom could have tracked and caught him, perhaps not. But at all events Tom had beaten him with character and that was enough. He had him and Thornton knew and confessed it. It *was* curious how it worked out, when you come to think of it.

Anyway, Thornton had given up all his fine plans and was ready to be arrested. He would tell the authorities that it was not on account of them that he gave himself up, but on account of Tom. Tom should have all the credit, as he deserved. He could hardly realize now that he had deliberately confessed to Tom. And having done so, he realized that Tom, being a good citizen, believing in the law and all that sort of thing, could not do otherwise than hand him over. What in the world else could Tom Slade do? Say to him, "You stole money; go ahead and escape; I'm with you?" Hardly.

There was a minute in Red Thornton's life when he came near making matters worse with a terrible blunder. After about fifteen or twenty minutes of waiting, he arose and stepped over to the gully and considered making a dash through the woods and striking into the road. Perhaps he would have done this; I cannot say. But happening just at that moment to glance down the hill in the opposite direction, he was astonished at seeing Tom plodding up the hill again quite alone. Neither Uncle Jeb nor any of those formidable scoutmasters or trustees were anywhere near him. Not so much as an uproarious, aggressive tenderfoot was at his heels. No constables, no deputy sheriffs, no one.

And then, just in that fleeting, perilous moment, Red Thornton knew Tom Slade and he knew that this was their business and no one else's. He came near to making an awful botch of things. He was breathing heavily when Tom spoke to him.

"What are those fellows you were speaking about? Pen and ink sleuths?" Tom asked. "They come to Temple Camp office, sometimes."

"That's them," Thornton said.

"When did you say they come?"

"Next Monday, first Monday in August. What's the difference? The sooner the better," Thornton said.

"Was it just an even hundred that you took, when you forgot about what you were doing, sort of?" Tom asked.

"A hundred and three."

"Then will twenty-three dollars be enough to get back to that place where you live?"

"Why?"

"I'm just asking you."

"It's twenty-one forty."

"That means you'll have a dollar sixty for meals," Tom said, "unless you have some of your own. Have you?"

Thornton seemed rather puzzled, but he jingled some coin in his pocket and pulled out a five dollar bill and some change.

"Then it's all right," Tom said, "'cause if I asked anybody for money I might have to tell them why. Here's two Liberty Bonds," he said, placing his precious, and much creased documents in Thornton's hand. "You can get them cashed in New York. You have to start this morning so as to catch the eleven twenty train. I guess you'll get home to-morrow night maybe, hey? You have to give them their money before those fellows get there. You got to tell them how you made a mistake. Maybe if you don't have quite enough you'll be able to get a little bit more. This is because you helped me and on account of our being friends."

Thornton looked down into his hand and saw, through glistening eyes, the two dilapidated bonds, and a couple of crumpled ten-dollar bills and some odds and ends of smaller bills and currency. They represented the sumptuous fortune of Lucky Luke, alias Tom Slade.

"And I thought you were going to ..." Thornton began; "Slady, I can't do this; it's all you've got."

"It's no good to me," Tom said. "Anyway, you got to go back and get there before those fellows do. Then you can fix it."

Thornton hesitated, then shook his head. Then he went over and sat on the sill where they had talked before. "I can't do it, Tom," he said finally; "I just can't. Here, take it. This is my affair, not yours."

"You said we were good friends up here," Tom said; "it's nothing to let a friend help you. I can see you're smart, and some day you'll make a lot of money and you'll pay me back. But anyway, I don't care about that. I only bought them so as to help the government. If they'd let me help them, I don't see why *you* shouldn't."

Thornton, still holding the money in his hand looked up and smiled, half willingly, at his singular argument.

"How about the motor-boat - and the girl?" he asked wistfully.

"You needn't worry about that," Tom said simply, "maybe she wouldn't go anyway."

And perhaps she wouldn't have. It would have been just his luck.

CHAPTER XXIX

TOM STARTS FOR HOME

There was nothing now to keep Tom at Temple Camp, yet there was nothing now to take him home, either. Nothing, indeed, except his work. The bottom seemed to have dropped out of all his plans, and he lingered on his lonely hilltop for the remaining day or two before the unsuspecting tenants of this remote little community should arrive.

Of course he might have stayed and enjoyed his triumph, but that would not have been Tom Slade. He had not forgotten those stinging and accusing words of Roy's that morning when they had last met. He did not remember them in malice, but he could not forget them, and he did not wish to see Roy. We have to take Tom Slade as we find him.

In those last hours of his lonely stay he did not go down much into camp, for he wished to be by himself, and not to have to answer questions about his departed friend, toward whom, strange to say, he cherished a stronger feeling of attachment than before. He was even grateful to Thornton for perhaps saving him the humiliation of Margaret Ellison's refusing to go out with him in his boat. There was no telling what a girl might say or do, and at least he was well out of that peril....

He busied himself clearing up the litter about the new cabins and getting them ready for occupancy. On Saturday morning he went down and told Uncle Jeb that he was starting for home. He was greatly relieved that the old man did not ask any questions about his companion. Uncle Jeb was much preoccupied now with the ever-growing multitude of scouts and their multifarious needs, and gave slight thought to that little sprig of a camp up on the hill.

"En so yer ain't fer stayin', Tommy? I kinder cal'lated you'd weaken when the time come. Ain't goin' ter think better of it, huh?" The old man, smiling through a cloud of tobacco smoke, contemplated Tom with shrewd, twinkling, expectant eyes. "Fun's jest about startin' naow, Tommy. 'Member what I told yer baot them critters. Daont yer go back on account of no gal."

"I ain't going back on account of a girl," said Tom.

"What train yer thinkin' uv goin' daon on?" the old man asked.

"I'm going to hike it," Tom said.

Uncle Jeb contemplated him for a moment as though puzzled, but after all, seeing nothing so very remarkable in a hike of a hundred and fifty miles or so, he simply observed. "Yer be'nt in no hurry ter get back, huh? Wall, yer better hev a good snack before yer start. You jest tell Chocolate Drop to put yer up rations fer ter night, too, in case you camp."

*   *   *   *   *

The guests at Temple Camp paid no particular attention to the young fellow who was leaving. He had not associated with the visiting scouts, and save for an occasional visit to his isolated retreat, where they found little to interest them, he had been almost a stranger among them. Doubtless some of them had thought him a mere workman at the camp and had left him undisturbed accordingly.

It was almost pitiful, now that he was leaving, to note how

slightly he was known and how little his departure affected the general routine of pleasure. A few scouts, who were diving from the spring board paused to glance at him as he rowed across the lake and observed that the "fellow from up on the hill" was going away. Others waved him a fraternal farewell, but there was none of that customary gathering at the landing, which he had known in the happy days when he had been a scout among scouts at his beloved camp.

But there was one scout who took enough interest in him to offer to go across in the rowboat with him, on the pretext of bringing it back, though both knew that it was customary to keep boats on both sides of the lake. This fellow was tall and of a quiet demeanor. His name was Archer, and he had come with his troop from somewhere in the west, where they breed that particular type of scouts who believe that actions speak louder than words.

"Did that job all by yourself, didn't you?" he asked as they rowed across. He looked a Tom curiously.

"A friend of mine helped me," Tom said; "he's gone home."

"Why didn't you hit into the main road and go down through Catskill? You're likely to miss the train this way."

"I'm going to hike home," Tom said.

"Far?"

"In Jersey, about twenty miles from the city."

"Some jaunt, eh?" Archer inquired pleasantly.

"I don't mind it," Tom said.

"What are you goin' home for?"

"Because I want to; because I'm finished," Tom said.

This ended the talk but it did not end Archer's rather curious study of Tom. He said little more, but as he rowed, he watched Tom with an intense and scrutinizing interest. And even after Tom had said good-bye to him and started up the trail through the woods, he rowed around, in the vicinity of the shore, keeping the boat in such position that he could follow Tom with his eyes as the latter followed the trail in and out among the trees.

"Humph," he said to himself; "funny."

What he thought funny was this: being an observant scout he had noticed that Tom carried more rations than a scout would be likely to take on a long hike, through a country where food could easily be bought in a hundred towns and villages, and also that one who limped as Tom did should choose to go on a hike of more than a hundred miles.

A scout, as everybody knows, is observant. And this particular scout was good at arithmetic. At least he was able to put two and two together....

CHAPTER XXX

THE TROOP ARRIVES

The ten forty-seven train out of New York went thundering up the shore of the lordly Hudson packed and jammed with its surging throng of vacationists who had turned themselves into sardines in order to enjoy a breath of fresh air. The crowd was uncommonly large because Saturday and the first of August came on the same day. They crowded three in a seat and ate sandwiches and drank cold coffee out of milk bottles and let the children fly paper-bag kites out of the windows, and crowded six deep at the water cooler at the end of the car.

In all that motley throng there was just one individual who had mastered the art of carrying a brimful paper drinking-cup through the aisle without spilling so much as a drop of water, and his cheerful ministrations were in great demand by thirsty passengers. This individual was scout Harris, alias Peewee, alias Kid, alias Shorty, alias Speck, and he was so small that he might have saved his carfare by going parcel post if he had cared to do so. If he had, he should have been registered, for there was only one Peewee Harris in all the wide world.

"Are we going to carry the tent or send it up by the camp wagon?" Roy Blakeley asked, as he and the others crowded each other off the train at Catskill Landing. "Answer in the positive or negative."

"You mean the infirmative," Peewee shouted; "that shows how

much you know about rhetoric."

"You mean logic," Roy said.

"I know I'm hungry anyway," Peewee shouted as he threw a suitcase from his vantage point on the platform, with such precision of aim that it landed plunk on Connie Bennett's head, to the infinite amusement of the passengers.

"Did it hurt you?" Peewee called.

"He isn't injured - just slightly killed," Roy shouted; "hurry up, let's go up in the wagon and get there in time for a light lunch."

"You mean a heavy one," Peewee yelled; "here, catch this suitcase."

The suitcase landed on somebody's head, was promptly hurled at somebody else, and the usual pandemonium caused by Temple Camp arrivals prevailed until the entire crowd of scouts found themselves packed in the big camp stage, and waving their hands and shouting uproariously at the passengers in the departing train.

"First season at camp?" Roy asked a scout who almost sat on his lap and was jogged out of place at every turn in the road.

"Yop," was the answer, "we've never been east before; we came from Ohio. We haven't been around anywhere."

"I've been around a lot," the irrepressible Peewee piped up from his wobbly seat on an up-ended suitcase.

"Sure, he was conductor on a merry-go-round," Roy said. "What part of Ohio do you fellows come from?"

"The Ohio River used to be in our geography," Peewee said.

"It's there yet," Roy said; "we should worry, let it stay there."

"Do you know where Columbus is?" Peewee shouted.

"He's dead," Roy said; "do you fellows come from anywhere near Dayton?"

"We come from Dansburg," said their scoutmaster, a bright-looking young fellow with red hair, who had been listening amusedly to this bantering talk.

A dead silence suddenly prevailed.

"Oh, I know who you fellows are," Roy finally said. "You're going to bunk in the three cabins on the hill, aren't you? Is your name Mr. Barnard?"

"Yes sir," the young man answered pleasantly, "and we're the first Dansburg, Ohio, troop."

"Do you like mince-pie?" Peewee shouted.

"We eat it alive," said scoutmaster Barnard.

"Can you eat seven pieces?" Peewee demanded.

"If we can get them," young Mr. Barnard replied.

"G - o - o - d night!" Peewee commented.

"Our young hero has a fine voice for eating," Roy observed. "Sometimes he eats his own words, he's so hungry."

"I don't think you can beat the Dansburg, Ohio, scouts eating," Mr. Barnard observed.

"Is Dansburg on the map?" Peewee wanted to know.

"Well, it thinks it is," Mr. Barnard smiled.

"I know all about geography," Peewee piped up, "and natural history, too. I got E plus in geometry."

"Can you name five animals that come from the North Pole?" Peewee demanded, regaining his seat after an inglorious tumble.

"Four polar bears and a seal," Roy answered; "no sooner said than stung. Our young hero is the camp cut-up. You fellows ought to be glad he won't be up on the hill with you. He's worse than the mosquitoes."

"We used to bunk in those cabins on the hill," Peewee said; "there are snakes and things up there. Are you scared of girls?"

"Not so you'd notice it," one of the Dansburg scouts said.

"Gee, I'm not scared of girls, that's one thing," Peewee informed them. "I'm not scared of any kind of wild animals."

"And would you call a girl a wild animal?" young Mr. Barnard inquired, highly amused.

"They scream when they get in a boat," Peewee said; "most always they smile at me."

"Oh, that's nothing, the first time I ever saw you I laughed out loud," Roy said.

And at that everybody laughed out loud, and somebody gave Peewee an apple which kept him quiet for a while.

"I'm very sorry we can't all be up on that hill together," Mr. Barnard said, "I gather that it's a rather isolated spot."

"What's an isolated spot?" Peewee yelled.

"It's a spot where they cut ice," said Roy; "shut up, will you?"

"Are there only three cabins up there?" one of the Dansville scouts wanted to know.

"That's all," Westy Martin, of Roy's troop answered. "We spent, let's see, three summers up there. We had the hill all to ourselves. We even did our own cooking."

"And eating," Peewee shouted.

"Oh sure, we never let anyone do that for us," one of the Bridgeboro scouts laughed.

"If you want a thing well done, do it yourself - especially eating," Roy said. "A scout is thorough."

"Do you know Chocolate Drop? He's cook," Peewee piped up. "He makes doughnuts as big as automobile tires."

"Not Cadillac tires," Roy said, "but Ford tires. Peewee knows how to puncture them, all right."

"He'll have a blow-out some day," Connie Bennett observed.

"So you boys used to be up on the hill, eh?" Mr. Barnard inquired, turning the conversation to a more serious vein. "And how is it you're not to bunk up there *this* year, since you like it so much?"

As if by common consent Roy's troop left it for him to answer, and even Peewee was quiet.

"Oh, I don't know," Roy said; "first come, first served; that's the rule. You fellows got in your application, that's all there was to it. I guess you know Tom Slade, who works in the camp's city office, don't you, Mr. Barnard?"

"Indeed I do," young Mr. Barnard said. "We met in a shell hole in France. We knew each other but have never seen each other. It's rather odd when you come to think of it."

"I suppose that's how he happened to assign you the cabins," Connie Bennett observed; "old time's sake, hey?"

"Oh, dear no," young Mr. Barnard laughed. "I should say that you boys come first if it's a question of old time's sake. No indeed, we should feel like intruders, usurpers, if there were any question of friendly preference. No, it was really quite odd when you come to think of it. I never dreamed who Tom Slade was when our accommodations were assigned us; indeed, his name did not appear in the correspondence. It was just a case of first come, first served, as you say. Later, we received some circular matter of the camp and there was a little note with it, as I remember, signed by Slade. Oh, no, the thing was all cut and dried before I knew who Slade was. Then we started a very pleasant correspondence. I expect to see him up here. He was one of the bravest young fellows on the west front; a sort of silent, taciturn, young fellow. Oh, no," young Mr. Barnard laughed in that pleasant way he had, "you boys can't accuse us of usurping your familiar home. You must come up and see us there, and I hope we shall all be good friends."

Roy Blakeley heard these words as in a dream, and even Peewee was silent. The others of Roy's troop looked at each other but said not a word. *No indeed, we should feel like usurpers if there were any question of friendly preference.* These words rang in Roy's ears, and as he said them over to himself there appeared in his mind's eye the picture of Tom Slade, stolid, unimpassioned, patient, unresentful - standing there near the doorway of the bank building and listening to the tirade of abuse which he, Roy, hurled at him. "*If you want to think I'm a liar you can think so. You can tell them that if you want to. I don't care what you tell them.*" These words, too, rang in Roy's ears, and burned into his heart and conscience, and he knew that Tom Slade had not deigned to answer these charges and recriminations; *would* not answer them, any more than the rock of Gibraltar would deign to answer the petulant threats and menaces of the sea. Oh, if he could only unsay those words which he had hurled at Tom, his friend and companion!

What mattered it who bunked in the cabins, so long as he knew what he knew now? How small and trifling seemed Tom's act of carelessness or forgetfulness, as he loomed up now in the strong, dogged pride which would not explain to one who had no right to doubt or disbelieve. How utterly contemptible Roy Blakeley seemed to himself now!

He tried to speak in his customary light and bantering manner, but he was too sick at heart to carry it off.

"He's - he's sort of like a rock," he said, by way of answering Barnard's comments on Tom. "He doesn't say much. You don't - you can't understand him very easy. Even - even *I* didn't -. I don't know where he is now. We haven't seen him for a long time. But one thing you can bet, you're welcome to the cabins on the hill. He said we wouldn't lose anything. Anyway, we won't lose much. We've got a tent we're going to put up down on the tenting space. You bet we'll come up and see you often, and you bet we'll be good friends. Our both knowing Tom, as you might say, ought to make us good friends."

CHAPTER XXXI

ARCHER

When these two troops reached camp they found the tall scout Archer waiting for them. How much he knew or suspected it would be difficult to surmise.

"Uncle Jeb told me I might show you up to the hill," he said. "Some of you fellows came from Ohio, I understand. You're all to bunk up on the hill."

"I guess that's a mistake," Roy said.

"No, I think Uncle Jeb has things down about pat," Archer said in his easy off-hand manner. "The old man's pretty busy himself and so he told me to be your guide, philosopher and friend, as old somebody-or-other said."

The two troops followed as he led the way, the Bridgeboro boys glancing fondly at the familiar sights all about them.

"There's where we'll put up our tent," one of them said, pointing at the area which was already crowded with the canvas domiciles. The place did not look so attractive as Roy and his companions had tried to picture it in their mind's eyes. They had never envied the scouts who had been compelled to make their camp homes there. It seemed so much like a military encampment, so close and stuffy and temporary, and unlike the free and remote abode that they were used to. They all of them tried not to think of it in this way, and Roy was in no mood to cherish any resentment against Tom now.

"It's near the cooking shack anyway, that's one good thing," Peewee observed.

"Listen to the human famine," Connie Bennett said. "Peewee ought to be ashamed to look Hoover in the face."

Roy said nothing. There was one he would be ashamed to look in the face anyway.

When they reached the hill, he was the first to pause in amazement.

"What do you call this?" Connie asked in utter astonishment.

There stood the six cabins, the new ones bright and fresh in the afternoon sun.

"I - I don't understand it," Roy said, almost speechless with surprise.

Archer sat down upon a rock and beckoned Roy to him. "There isn't much to tell you," he said. "A fellow from your town has been up here building these three cabins, that's all. We fellows down at camp called him Daniel Boone, but I believe his name is Slade. He's been a kind of a mystery up here for some time. The cabins are for you and your troop, there's no mistake about that; Uncle Jeb knows all about it. You can see him later if you want to; there's no use bothering him now. I just want to say a word to you there isn't much time to spare. Uncle Jeb tried to make that fellow stay, but he wouldn't. I don't know anything about his business, or yours. I'm just going to tell you one thing. That fellow started away a little while ago, lame and without any money to hike home to the town where he lives. It's none of *my* business; I'm just telling you what I know. I've banged around this country a little since I came up - I'm a kind of a tramp - I have an idea he's hit into the road for Kingston. There's a short cut through the woods which comes out on that road about six or seven miles down. You could save - let's see - oh, about three miles and - oh, yes, Uncle Jeb told me to say you can have lunch any time you want it. I suppose you're all hungry."

Not another word did Archer say - just left abruptly and, amid the enthusiastic inspection and glowing comments of his companions of both troops, Roy saw, through glistening eyes, this new acquaintance strolling down the hill, hitting the wildflowers to the right, and left with a stick which he carried.

There was no telling how much he knew or what he suspected. He was a queer, mysterious sort of fellow....

CHAPTER XXXII

TOM LOSES

"*Me for lunch! Me for lunch!*" Roy heard Peewee scream at the top of his voice. And for just a moment he stood there in a kind of daze, watching his companions and new friends tumbling pell mell over each other down the hill. He was glad to be alone.

Yet even still he paused and gazed at the task, which Tom Slade, traitor and liar, had completed. There it was, a herculanean task, the work of months, as it seemed to Roy. He could hardly control his feelings as he gazed upon it.

But he did not pause to torture himself with remorse. Down through the woods he went, and into the trail which Archer had indicated. Scout though he was, he was never less hungry in his life. Over fields he went, and through the brook, and up Hawk's Nest mountain, and into the denser woods beyond. Suppose Archer should be mistaken. Suppose this dim trail should take him nowhere. Panting, he ran on, trying to conquer this haunting fear. Beyond Leeds Crossing the trail was hardly distinguishable and he must pause and lose time to pick it up here and there. Through woods, and around hills, and into dense, almost impenetrable thickets he labored on, his side aching, and his heart thumping like a triphammer.

At last he came out upon the Kingston road and was down on his knees, examining minutely every mark in the dusty road, trying to determine whether Tom had passed. Then he sat down by the roadside and waited, panting like a dog. And so the minutes passed, and became an hour and -

Then he heard someone coming around the bend.

Roy gulped in suspense as he waited. One second, two seconds, three, four - Would the pedestrian never appear?

And then they met, and Roy Blakeley stood out in the middle of the road and held his arms out so the wayfarer could not pass. And yet he could not speak.

"Tom," he finally managed to say, "I - I came alone because - because I wanted to come alone. I wanted to meet you all alone. I - I know all about it, Tom - I do. None of the fellows will bunk in these cabins till you - till you - come back - they won't. Not even Barnard's troop. I'm sorry, Tom; I see how I was all wrong. You - you can't get away with it, you can't Tom - because I won't let you - see? You have to come back - we - we can't stay there without you -"

"I told you you wouldn't lose anything," Tom said dully.

"Yes, and it's a - it's a *lie*," Roy almost sobbed. "We're losing *you*, aren't we? We're losing everything - and it's all *my* fault. You - you said we wouldn't lose anything, but we *are*. Can't you see we are? You've got to come back, Tom - or I'm going home with you - you old - you old brick! Barnard wants you, we *all* want you. We haven't got any scoutmaster if you don't come back - we haven't."

Tom Slade who had chopped down trees and dragged them up the hill, found it hard to answer.

"I'll go back," he finally said, "as long as you ask me."

*   *   *   *   *

And so, in that pleasant afternoon, they followed the trail back to camp together, just as they had hiked together so many times before. And they talked of Peewee and the troop and joked about there not being anything left to eat when they got there, and Roy said what a fine fellow Barnard was, and Tom Slade said how he always liked fellows with red hair. He said he thought you could trust them....

Let us hope he was right.

Choose from Thousands of 1stWorldLibrary Classics By

A. M. Barnard
Ada Leverson
Adolphus William Ward
Aesop
Agatha Christie
Alexander Aaronsohn
Alexander Kielland
Alexandre Dumas
Alfred Gatty
Alfred Ollivant
Alice Duer Miller
Alice Turner Curtis
Alice Dunbar
Allen Chapman
Ambrose Bierce
Amelia E. Barr
Amory H. Bradford
Andrew Lang
Andrew McFarland Davis
Andy Adams
Anna Alice Chapin
Anna Sewell
Annie Besant
Annie Hamilton Donnell
Annie Payson Call
Annie Roe Carr
Annonaymous
Anton Chekhov
Arnold Bennett
Arthur Conan Doyle
Arthur M. Winfield
Arthur Ransome
Arthur Schnitzler
Atticus
B.H. Baden-Powell
B. M. Bower
B. C. Chatterjee
Baroness Emmuska Orczy
Baroness Orczy
Basil King
Bayard Taylor
Ben Macomber
Bertha Muzzy Bower
Bjornstjerne Bjornson
Booth Tarkington
Boyd Cable
Bram Stoker
C. Collodi
C. E. Orr

C. M. Ingleby
Carolyn Wells
Catherine Parr Traill
Charles A. Eastman
Charles Amory Beach
Charles Dickens
Charles Dudley Warner
Charles Farrar Browne
Charles Ives
Charles Kingsley
Charles Klein
Charles Hanson Towne
Charles Lathrop Pack
Charles Romyn Dake
Charles Whibley
Charles Willing Beale
Charlotte M. Braeme
Charlotte M. Yonge
Charlotte Perkins Stetson
Clair W. Hayes
Clarence Day Jr.
Clarence E. Mulford
Clemence Housman
Confucius
Coningsby Dawson
Cornelis DeWitt Wilcox
Cyril Burleigh
D. H. Lawrence
Daniel Defoe
David Garnett
Dinah Craik
Don Carlos Janes
Donald Keyhoe
Dorothy Kilner
Dougan Clark
Douglas Fairbanks
E. Nesbit
E.P.Roe
E. Phillips Oppenheim
Earl Barnes
Edgar Rice Burroughs
Edith Van Dyne
Edith Wharton
Edward Everett Hale
Edward J. O'Biren
Edward S. Ellis
Edwin L. Arnold
Eleanor Atkins
Eliot Gregory

Elizabeth Gaskell
Elizabeth McCracken
Elizabeth Von Arnim
Ellem Key
Emerson Hough
Emilie F. Carlen
Emily Dickinson
Enid Bagnold
Enilor Macartney Lane
Erasmus W. Jones
Ernie Howard Pie
Ethel May Dell
Ethel Turner
Ethel Watts Mumford
Eugenie Foa
Eugene Wood
Eustace Hale Ball
Evelyn Everett-green
Everard Cotes
F. H. Cheley
F. J. Cross
F. Marion Crawford
Federick Austin Ogg
Ferdinand Ossendowski
Francis Bacon
Francis Darwin
Frances Hodgson Burnett
Frances Parkinson Keyes
Frank Gee Patchin
Frank Harris
Frank Jewett Mather
Frank L. Packard
Frank V. Webster
Frederic Stewart Isham
Frederick Trevor Hill
Frederick Winslow Taylor
Friedrich Kerst
Friedrich Nietzsche
Fyodor Dostoyevsky
G.A. Henty
G.K. Chesterton
Gabrielle E. Jackson
Garrett P. Serviss
Gaston Leroux
George A. Warren
George Ade
Geroge Bernard Shaw
George Durston
George Ebers

George Eliot
George Gissing
George MacDonald
George Meredith
George Orwell
George Sylvester Viereck
George Tucker
George W. Cable
George Wharton James
Gertrude Atherton
Gordon Casserly
Grace E. King
Grace Gallatin
Grace Greenwood
Grant Allen
Guillermo A. Sherwell
Gulielma Zollinger
Gustav Flaubert
H. A. Cody
H. B. Irving
H.C. Bailey
H. G. Wells
H. H. Munro
H. Irving Hancock
H. Rider Haggard
H. W. C. Davis
Haldeman Julius
Hall Caine
Hamilton Wright Mabie
Hans Christian Andersen
Harold Avery
Harold McGrath
Harriet Beecher Stowe
Harry Castlemon
Harry Coghill
Harry Houidini
Hayden Carruth
Helent Hunt Jackson
Helen Nicolay
Hendrik Conscience
Hendy David Thoreau
Henri Barbusse
Henrik Ibsen
Henry Adams
Henry Ford
Henry Frost
Henry James
Henry Jones Ford
Henry Seton Merriman
Henry W Longfellow
Herbert A. Giles

Herbert Carter
Herbert N. Casson
Herman Hesse
Hildegard G. Frey
Homer
Honore De Balzac
Horace B. Day
Horace Walpole
Horatio Alger Jr.
Howard Pyle
Howard R. Garis
Hugh Lofting
Hugh Walpole
Humphry Ward
Ian Maclaren
Inez Haynes Gillmore
Irving Bacheller
Isabel Hornibrook
Israel Abrahams
Ivan Turgenev
J.G.Austin
J. Henri Fabre
J. M. Barrie
J. Macdonald Oxley
J. S. Fletcher
J. S. Knowles
J. Storer Clouston
Jack London
Jacob Abbott
James Allen
James Andrews
James Baldwin
James Branch Cabell
James DeMille
James Joyce
James Lane Allen
James Lane Allen
James Oliver Curwood
James Oppenheim
James Otis
James R. Driscoll
Jane Austen
Jane L. Stewart
Janet Aldridge
Jens Peter Jacobsen
Jerome K. Jerome
John Burroughs
John Cournos
John F. Kennedy
John Gay
John Glasworthy

John Habberton
John Joy Bell
John Kendrick Bangs
John Milton
John Philip Sousa
Jonas Lauritz Idemil Lie
Jonathan Swift
Joseph A. Altsheler
Joseph Carey
Joseph Conrad
Joseph E. Badger Jr
Joseph Hergesheimer
Joseph Jacobs
Jules Vernes
Julian Hawthrone
Julie A Lippmann
Justin Huntly McCarthy
Kakuzo Okakura
Kenneth Grahame
Kenneth McGaffey
Kate Langley Bosher
Kate Langley Bosher
Katherine Cecil Thurston
Katherine Stokes
L. A. Abbot
L. T. Meade
L. Frank Baum
Latta Griswold
Laura Dent Crane
Laura Lee Hope
Laurence Housman
Lawrence Beasley
Leo Tolstoy
Leonid Andreyev
Lewis Carroll
Lewis Sperry Chafer
Lilian Bell
Lloyd Osbourne
Louis Hughes
Louis Tracy
Louisa May Alcott
Lucy Fitch Perkins
Lucy Maud Montgomery
Luther Benson
Lydia Miller Middleton
Lyndon Orr
M. Corvus
M. H. Adams
Margaret E. Sangster
Margret Howth
Margaret Vandercook

Margret Penrose
Maria Edgeworth
Maria Thompson Daviess
Mariano Azuela
Marion Polk Angellotti
Mark Overton
Mark Twain
Mary Austin
Mary Catherine Crowley
Mary Cole
Mary Hastings Bradley
Mary Roberts Rinehart
Mary Rowlandson
M. Wollstonecraft Shelley
Maud Lindsay
Max Beerbohm
Myra Kelly
Nathaniel Hawthrone
Nicolo Machiavelli
O. F. Walton
Oscar Wilde
Owen Johnson
P.G. Wodehouse
Paul and Mabel Thorne
Paul G. Tomlinson
Paul Severing
Percy Brebner
Peter B. Kyne
Plato
R. Derby Holmes
R. L. Stevenson
R. S. Ball
Rabindranath Tagore
Rahul Alvares
Ralph Bonehill
Ralph Henry Barbour
Ralph Victor
Ralph Waldo Emmerson
Rene Descartes
Rex Beach

Rex E. Beach
Richard Harding Davis
Richard Jefferies
Richard Le Gallienne
Robert Barr
Robert Frost
Robert Gordon Anderson
Robert L. Drake
Robert Lansing
Robert Lynd
Robert Michael Ballantyne
Robert W. Chambers
Rosa Nouchette Carey
Rudyard Kipling
Samuel B. Allison
Samuel Hopkins Adams
Sarah Bernhardt
Sarah C. Hallowell
Selma Lagerlof
Sherwood Anderson
Sigmund Freud
Standish O'Grady
Stanley Weyman
Stella Benson
Stella M. Francis
Stephen Crane
Stewart Edward White
Stijn Streuvels
Swami Abhedananda
Swami Parmananda
T. S. Ackland
T. S. Arthur
The Princess Der Ling
Thomas A. Janvier
Thomas A Kempis
Thomas Anderton
Thomas Bailey Aldrich
Thomas Bulfinch
Thomas De Quincey
Thomas Dixon

Thomas H. Huxley
Thomas Hardy
Thomas More
Thornton W. Burgess
U. S. Grant
Valentine Williams
Various Authors
Vaughan Kester
Victor Appleton
Victoria Cross
Virginia Woolf
Wadsworth Camp
Walter Camp
Walter Scott
Washington Irving
Wilbur Lawton
Wilkie Collins
Willa Cather
Willard F. Baker
William Dean Howells
William le Queux
W. Makepeace Thackeray
William W. Walter
William Shakespeare
Winston Churchill
Yei Theodora Ozaki
Yogi Ramacharaka
Young E. Allison
Zane Grey

www.ingramcontent.com/pod-product-compliance
Lightning Source LLC
Chambersburg PA
CBHW030755150426
42813CB00068B/3124/J